Pg.60 *
Pg.62 *
178
180
182 *
185 *
189 *
192 *
* 203 *
204
Pg.69

PLAY IT!

Zondervan/Youth Specialties Books

Adventure Games
Amazing Tension Getters
Attention Grabbers for 4th–6th Graders (Get 'Em Growing)
Called to Care
The Complete Student Missions Handbook
Creative Socials and Special Events
Divorce Recovery for Teenagers
Feeding Your Forgotten Soul
Get 'Em Talking!
Good Clean Fun
Good Clean Fun, Volume 2
Great Games for 4th–6th Graders (Get 'Em Growing)
Great Ideas for Small Youth Groups
Greatest Skits on Earth
Greatest Skits on Earth, Volume 2
Growing Up in America
High School Ministry
High School TalkSheets
Holiday Ideas for Youth Groups (Revised Edition)
Hot Talks
Ideas for Social Action
Intensive Care: Helping Teenagers in Crisis
Junior High Ministry
Junior High TalkSheets
The Ministry of Nurture
On-Site: 40 On-Location Programs for Youth Groups
Option Plays
Organizing Your Youth Ministry
Play It! Great Games for Groups
Teaching the Bible Creatively
Teaching the Truth about Sex
Tension Getters
Tension Getters II
Unsung Heroes: How to Recruit and Train Volunteer Youth Workers
Up Close and Personal: How to Build Community in Your Youth Group
Youth Specialties Clip Art Book
Youth Specialties Clip Art Book, Volume 2

PLAY IT!

OVER 400 GREAT GAMES FOR GROUPS

Wayne Rice and Mike Yaconelli
Illustrations by Dan Pegoda

Youth Specialties

ZondervanPublishingHouse
Grand Rapids, Michigan

A Division of HarperCollinsPublishers

PLAY IT!
Copyright © 1986 by Youth Specialties, Inc.

Requests for information should be addressed to:
Zondervan Publishing House
Grand Rapids, Michigan 49530

Library of Congress Cataloging in Publication Data

Rice, Wayne
    Play It!

    Includes index.
    l. Group games. 2. Cooperativeness. I. Yaconelli, Mike. II. Title.
    GV1201.R4435 1986   790.1'5   86-13208
    ISBN 0-310-35191-X

Edited by David Lambert
Designed by Ann Cherryman
Illustrated by Dan Pegoda

Printed in the United States of America

95 96 97 / CH / 19

The games in this book originally appeared in the *Ideas* Library, published by Youth Specialties, Inc.

The authors wish to thank all of the creative youth workers who originally developed these games and who contributed them for publication. Without them, this book would not have been possible.

CONTENTS

1.

PLAY IT!

This is a game book.

But it is no *ordinary* game book.

Play It! is a book packed full of games that people—all kinds of people—will want to play. This may sound surprising in a society that has allowed almost all game playing to become something you *watch*— a pressurized, highly competitive battleground where winning is everything and people don't matter. *Play It!* was written because we believe people want to play games again and want to have fun. So we have chosen games that are not only fun but are also playable by nearly everyone—games that are an occasion for celebration, not warfare.

We chose the games in *Play It!* by using specific criteria that have nothing to do with winning or with skill. Instead, every game was chosen for its potential in building community.

Not that competition is inherently evil. A good game has to involve some form of competition. But *winning* should never be the focus of game playing. Winning should be either irrelevant or anticlimactic. Competition is useful when it increases the enjoyment of those who are playing. When competition results in driving a wedge between the "good" and the "bad" or the "skilled" and the "nonskilled," then it becomes a detriment to game playing.

Just as enjoyment is more important than competition, participation is more important than observation or performance. Games were made to be played, not watched. Yet many of us have willingly accepted the role of spectator rather than participator. In fact, many of us seem to be reluctant to participate actively in a game because we think we're not good enough. We're afraid of ridicule or embarrassment. The result is that games have become the private domain of the athlete and the professional. It's time we reclaimed game playing for all of us, so we can experience play firsthand rather than vicariously. We need to change people's orientation "from 'instant replay' to 'instant we-play.'"[1]

When winning is the bottom line, the only ones who enjoy the game are those on the winning team and those who feel like they contributed to the win with a great performance. When each player's participation is the bottom line, then everyone can enjoy the game itself, whether they win or lose, because merely *playing* the game gives them pleasure.

Cooperative community should *always* be the goal of playing games. After a game is over, players should be better friends than when the game started. That should be the result of every game we play.

It takes little effort to change our orientation from competition to cooperation. Once we decide never to let winning get in the way of a relationship, we can begin to see the other person as an ally rather than as the enemy. Cooperating in a game does not mean that we do not compete; it simply means that we never let competition get in the way of our relationship with everyone else in the game.

There are over four hundred games in this book. Now, you won't have to worry about finding a game to play. Instead, you will have to decide *which* game to play. There are more games in this book than you'll ever need. That's a good problem to have—but how do you decide which is the "right" game for you?

HOW TO CHOOSE THE RIGHT GAME

A right game is a game that works for your particular group of players. A wrong game is a game that doesn't work for your group. How do you tell which games will work and which won't? Here are some of the things to consider:

[1] Matt Weinstein, Joel Goodman, *Playfair* (Impact, 1983), p. 24.

1. Safety

Any game is wrong if people are likely to be hurt. Of course, any game *can* result in an accidental injury. But sometimes people are hurt because reasonable precautions were not taken. When you as a leader present a game to others, they assume you have taken every precaution for their safety. Here are some safety suggestions for any game you play:

a. Make sure that you have played—or have watched someone else play—any game that you decide to use with others.

b. Take extra precautions when very small children or the elderly are playing with you.

c. Do not encourage players to play rough.

d. Check the location of your game for protruding objects, hard surfaces, obstacles, slippery floors, or any hazard that might endanger one of the players.

e. If you change or adapt a game, make sure you think through the implications of those changes.

f. Athletes are athletes—they enjoy competition and they enjoy winning. You may find the more athletic players dominating a game by playing too aggressively. Encourage the more athletic types not to dominate the play. If the athletes continue to play too roughly, you may have to give the athletes some kind of handicap, such as hopping on one leg or using only their left hands.

g. Double check your insurance coverage to make sure all injuries will be covered adequately.

h. Always have adequate first aid equipment on hand.

i. When you sponsor a large, day-long game event with young people, it's a good idea to require parental release forms, so that immediate care can be given to those who are injured.

NOTE: Make every effort to include the handicapped in your game playing. Too often, people automatically assume the handicapped cannot play when just a minor adjustment to the rules would make it possible for them to join the game. And even when a person's handicaps are very severe, you may still be able to include him—why not make him a referee, the official game photographer, or the scorekeeper?

2. Age of Group

Almost every game in this book may be played by any person, regardless of age. But there are certain games that are more suitable for specific ages. If you need a game for families, choose one that involves cooperation and little physical contact. If you're choosing games for high school guys, choose high-energy games with lots of physical contact.

3. Sex

In spite of legitimate concerns about sexism, it is usually best to separate the sexes for physical, hard-hitting games. This doesn't mean that girls can't play physical games; it simply means that *some* games are played best if they are not played co-ed.

4. Size

Some games, like JOHN-JOHN (page 150), don't play very well with a small group; others, like ANATOMY SHUFFLE (page 66), work fine. Before game time, consider how the games you choose will work with your size of group.

5. Personality

Every group has a unique personality—its group dynamics. Some groups are active, outgoing, and physical, while others are more easygoing or sophisticated. It's good to give a group new experiences; it's also good to *start* with a game that the group feels comfortable with. The secret is not to choose games solely on the basis of whether *you* enjoy them. Rather, choose games that your *group* will find enjoyable.

6. Ability

There are some things certain people can't do. For example, little children have a hard time balancing cups of water on their heads; older people have a more difficult time hopping around a football field. Take into account the ability of your group when planning any game.

7. Purpose

The overall purpose of every game is to build community and to have fun. But beyond that, games can serve many purposes: wearing out restless campers on the first and last nights of camp; helping people become better acquainted; or providing good healthy exercise. The point is that games can do more than provide enjoyment; they can accomplish other worthwhile purposes at the same time.

Remember that games are for people, and no two people experience games in exactly the same way. These guidelines will not insure that every game you play will work perfectly, but they will help.

ADAPTABILITY

Games may be played anywhere, anytime, with anyone. Even so, every group has at least one person who can't play a game unless he plays by the official rules on an official field with official equipment. It's true that many games are best played under *official* conditions; however, any game may be adapted to fit *any* set of circumstances. Adaptability simply means that games were meant to be played, and that whatever has to be done to get people to play and enjoy themselves should be done.

1. Adapting the Rules. Rules tell you how to play a game a certain way. That doesn't mean you can't play the game a different way. If the rules are getting in the way of the game, then change them to make the game better. For example, if your group is playing baseball and no one can hit the ball because the pitching is too fast, just make a rule that pitches have to be slow. Remember, playing games is supposed to be fun.

2. Adapting the Time. Time isn't really that important. As long as people are having fun, time limits are irrelevant. You are free to interrupt or shorten a game if it's boring; you are free to lengthen a game if everyone is enjoying it. Time can be an asset to game playing if *you* control the time rather than letting *it* control you.

3. Adapting the Weather. Well—not really. You can't change the weather, but you can change the game to accommodate the weather. For example, you can't keep it from raining on your volleyball game, but you can still play volleyball in the rain, play volleyball with umbrellas, or play mud volleyball. Bad weather, within reason (you obviously can't play during a tornado or blizzard), should never stop a game, rather it should simply cause you to adapt your game to the weather.

4. Adapting the Equipment. Almost every game requires some kind of equipment. You should, of course, always try to get the kind of equipment that will contribute to the best play possible. But you aren't a slave to equipment. If you can't find a volleyball, use a soccer ball, four square ball, or whatever you can find. If what you find looks like it will affect the outcome of the game, then change the rules. You can play broom hockey with a volleyball, soccer ball, grapefruit (yes, grapefruit), or even two T-shirts wadded up.

HOW TO PLAY A GAME

You can't tell others how to play a game if you haven't played the game or seen it played. You should be able to explain a game simply, clearly, and as quickly as possible. Rather than letting people ask a million "what-if" questions, just play the game. Most questions are answered while actually playing the practice rounds. But if the basic rules and instructions of the game aren't understood by everyone, the result may be mass confusion. That means you must have everyone's attention while explaining the game. Never try to shout directions over the noise of an inattentive group. Use a bullhorn or public address system for large groups. For somewhat smaller groups, a good referee's whistle (inexpensive whistles are never loud enough) or marine boat horn (keep the boat horn in a secure place because if it's pointed toward a person's ear at close range, it can do some serious damage) will get their attention. It's a good idea when you are playing games with large

15

groups to have a permanent rule: Whenever the horn or whistle is sounded, everyone must sit down immediately and be quiet.

When you have the attention of the group, explain the game clearly and enthusiastically. Make your explanation sound like as much fun as playing the game itself. Demonstrate exactly how the game is to be played. (It's usually easier to *show* the group how to play than it is to *tell* them how to play.)

CHOOSING TEAMS

If you use a game requiring teams, remember that choosing teams embarrasses those who have the misfortune of being chosen last, especially if they're *always* last or think they are. The best option is to use a game like "Barnyard," which automatically puts everyone into groups. These groups can then become teams before anyone realizes what happened.

Most of the games in *Play It!* do not require normal abilities (holding an egg in your armpit?), so the quality of the team is not determined by size, strength, or athletic ability. All you need for a good team is a group of people who want to play.

REFEREES

Every game requires several responsible people to help conduct and supervise the games, especially when large groups of people are involved. A good ratio is one leader for every twenty players. Make sure the referees are well-identified with striped jerseys, fluorescent jackets, or bright hats. Make certain that all the referees thoroughly understand the rules of the game. Practice the game first with a test group to work out any situations not explained in the rules. If the referees have to keep referring to the book, they are not familiar enough with the game.

There are two kinds of referees. First, the Letter-of-the-Law type.

He believes referees are authority figures, whose main function is to enforce the rules—to the letter. Those kinds of referees are fine in the NFL, but not anywhere else.

The second kind of referee is the Fun-and-Games type. This kind of referee understands that rules are nothing more than guidelines to make a game fun and enjoyable. He understands that an infraction occurs when people's enjoyment of the game is in jeopardy. So, if one team is desperately behind, the referee becomes more observant of the winning team and less observant of the team that is behind. The Fun-and-Games referee recognizes that rules exist for the benefit of the people playing the game, rather than the people existing for the benefit of the rules.

POINTS

Many groups use points to tabulate the standings of teams during game events. As silly as it may sound, the amount of points you give can actually increase the enjoyment and excitement of those who are playing. Points are free, so you don't have to be stingy with them. Give *lots* of points—a thousand points! Three thousand points! After all, who wants to play a game for fifty measly points when he can win three thousand points? Live a little—give ten thousand points!

Now that we have the preliminaries out of the way, you can start doing what you're supposed to be doing—playing. We honestly hope that, from now on, the games you play will be fun and enjoyable, and that they will bring you closer to the people you play with. We sincerely hope that *Play It!* will help you rediscover the *joy* of game playing.

2.

OUTDOOR GAMES
FOR
LARGE GROUPS

This chapter contains a variety of outdoor games for groups of thirty or more. Some can be played with an almost unlimited number of people. They are best played on a large, open field.

Keep in mind that there are many other games in this book that can also be played outdoors with large groups. The relays in chapter 7, for example, can be used with any size group, and many of the indoor games in chapter 4 can be adapted for outdoor use. Don't limit yourself to this chapter if you are looking for that "just right" game for your next outdoor activity.

AMOEBA

For this game, you will need several long, stout ropes. Divide into teams of any size. Simply tie a rope around the entire team at the waists. Have the team bunch up together as closely as they can and hold their arms up while you tie the rope around them. After they are tied, they can race to a goal and back. Unless they work together as a team, they will fall down or go nowhere. It's a riot to watch.

A-B-C'S

This game is good for large groups of forty or more. Divide into teams. The leader must position himself high above the kids, like up on a roof or mountain, so he can see all the kids below. He then shouts a letter of the alphabet, and each team must form that letter as quickly as possible (like a marching band would do). The first team to form the letter wins. Teams may also be judged for the best formation of the letter in case of ties.

AMERICAN EAGLE

This is not a coed game. All guys or all girls line up on a line. They choose one who stands thirty feet or so away in the middle of a field.

When the whistle is blown, players start running toward the guy in the middle of the field. That guy tackles one (or more if he can), holds him down, and says, "American Eagle" three times. Now the rest of the players are on the other side of the field and must run through two guys to get back to the original side again. The game continues until everybody has been tackled and is in the middle of the field. Give a prize to the last runner.

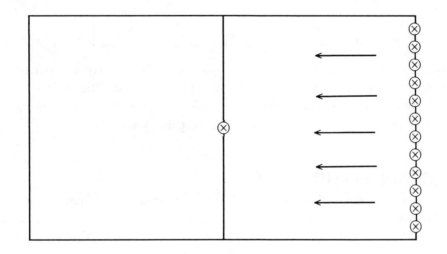

BEDLAM

This game requires four teams of equal size. Each team takes one corner of the room or playing field. The play area can be either square or rectangular. At a signal (whistle, etc.), each team attempts to move as quickly as possible to the corner directly across from them (diagonally), performing an announced activity as they go. The first team to get all its members into its new corner wins that particular round. The first round can be simply running to the opposite corner, but after that you can use

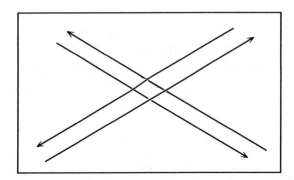

any number of possibilities, such as walking backward, wheelbarrow racing (one person is the wheelbarrow), piggyback, rolling somersaults, hopping on one foot, skipping, and crab walking. There will be mass bedlam in the center as all four teams crisscross.

BEDLAM ELIMINATION

This game is a good variation of the previous one. Team members gather in the four corners of the playing field as before, but this time each person gets a flag (like those used in flag football) that they must wear in their pants. A safe area is designated with a line for each team, and the game begins with everyone behind that line.

On "go," everyone races across the field to the opposite corner, but on the way, tries to grab the flag out of an opposing team member's pants. If successful, the team gets a point for the captured flag, and the team member who lost his flag is eliminated from the game. Play continues until only members of one team are left, and that team is the winner.

THE BLOB

Clearly mark off boundaries and put spotters on the corners. During the course of the game, anyone who steps outside the boundaries becomes part of the blob.

One person begins as the blob. The blob then tries to tag or chase one of the other players. If another player is tagged or is chased out-of-bounds, that person becomes part of the blob. These two join hands and go after a third person who, when tagged, joins hands and helps tag a fourth. The game continues until everyone is part of the blob. The blob's only restriction is that it cannot break hands. Thus, only people on the ends can make legal tags.

For the blob to be most effective, it must work as a unit. One person should act as the "blob brain" and control The Blob. No tags count if the blob becomes separated, so the blob must go after one person at a time. Once the blob becomes large enough, it can stretch across the playing field and catch everyone.

CAPTURE THE FLAG

This is an old game, but one that kids always love to play. The playing field needs to resemble this diagram:

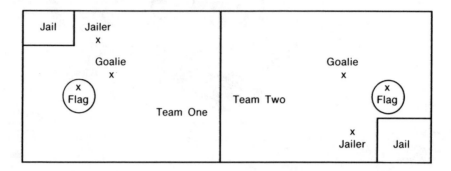

Team 1 is on one side of the field, and Team 2 is on the other side. The idea of the game is to capture the flag, located in the other team's territory, without getting tagged (or tackled, clobbered, etc.). Once you cross over the line in the middle of the field, you can be tagged and sent to the jail by each team's flag. If you are in jail, one of your teammates can free you by getting to the jail without getting tagged and then tagging you. You both get a free walk back to safety. Each team has one goalie who watches the flag from a distance of about ten feet and a jailer who guards the jail. The idea is to work out some strategy with your teammates to rush the flag or to capture the flag and then run it across the line.

CAPTURE THE FOOTBALL

If you are playing "Capture the Flag" with high schoolers, or with boys only, you might try this exciting variation. Use footballs instead of flags. You can pass or run the ball over the line to win. If you are tagged (or tackled if you want a rougher version), you must remain a prisoner until a teammate tags you and sets you free. If you pass the ball to a teammate over the line that separates the two territories and your teammate drops the pass, you both become prisoners and go to jail. If the pass is complete, then you win. You can adapt the other Capture the Flag rules as you see fit.

CAR STUFF

For this wild game, you need a car that can risk possible damage and dirt. Kids line up on one side of the car with both front or back doors open and at a signal run through the car (in one side and out the other). After going through the car, the players return to the end of the line and run through again until the time limit is up. Each team has a timer and a counter, and the object is to see how many kids can run through the car in the time limit (one minute, two minutes, etc.). Each team gets a try. To play this game without using a car, use a large cardboard box, a bench that the kids must crawl under, or simply have three guys stand in a row with their legs spread, and the team must crawl under their legs.

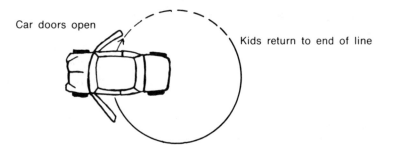

Car doors open

Kids return to end of line

ELIMINATION VOLLEYBALL

Here is another version of volleyball that is a lot of fun. Divide your group into two teams and play a regular volleyball game, but whoever makes a mistake or misses the ball goes out of the game. The teams keep getting smaller and smaller, and the team that manages to survive the longest is the winner.

FAT BAT

Here's a version of softball that can be played out-of-doors in any kind of weather. Anybody can play. It doesn't require much skill.

You'll need to purchase a fat bat and fat ball from a toy store or department store. They are relatively easy to find and quite inexpensive. Regular softball rules apply, only there are no foul balls. Everything is fair. Players don't use ball gloves. The ball is so light that a good wind will carry it everywhere. So the nastier the weather, the better.

FOUR TEAM VOLLEYBALL

Here's a wild version of volleyball that involves four teams at once. You can set it up with four volleyball nets or just two, depending on the size of your teams and the number of nets you have available. You'll also need five or six poles. Arrange the nets according to one of the diagrams below. If you use two nets, then you form two right angles with them, as in diagram A. If you use four nets, tie all four to the center pole, as in diagram B.

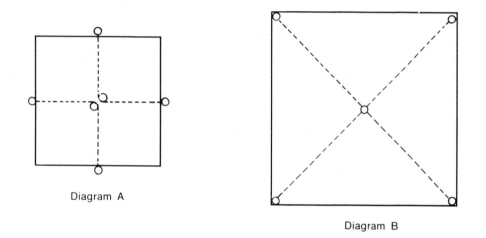

Diagram A

Diagram B

The four teams get in one of the four corners of the court, and the game is played like regular volleyball, except now you can hit the ball to any of the other three teams. An interesting strategy can develop since a team is never sure exactly when the ball will be coming their way.

Once you try this version of volleyball, your group may never want to play regular volleyball again!

FRIS BALL

This game is played like softball with any number of players. However, a Frisbee is used instead of a bat and ball. Also, each team should get six outs instead of three. The Frisbee must go at least thirty feet on a fly or it is foul. The offensive team does not have to wait until the defensive team is ready before sending their batter to the plate. This keeps the normal between-innings slowdown to a minimum.

HORSEYBACK TAG

This is a wild game that should be played on a grassy area. Each team is made up of a horse and rider. The rider mounts the horse by jumping on the back of the horse with arms around the horse's neck. The riders have a piece of masking tape placed on their backs by the leader to be seen and reached easily. When the signal "mount up" is given, the riders mount their horses and attempt to round up the tape on the other riders' backs. The last rider left with tape on his back wins. Only the riders may take the tape off other riders (the horses are just horses), and if a horse falls, then that horse and rider are out of the game.

HUMAN FOOTBALL

Here's a wild game that can be played on any rectangular playing field, outdoors or indoors. A normal football field works fine. There are two teams, the offense and the defense. There can be any number of boys or girls on each team.

When a team is on offense, they begin at the 20-yard line. They get four downs to move the ball down the field and to score a touchdown. There are no additional first downs. The way yardage is made is for the team on offense to hike the ball to its quarterback who is then picked up and carried by the rest of the team down the field. The entire team must be joined together, either by carrying the quarterback or by holding on to team members who are carrying the quarterback.

The defensive team begins each play lined up on the goal line that they are defending. As soon as the offensive team hikes the ball, the defensive team locks arms and walks down the field toward the offensive team moving toward them. When the defensive team reaches the offensive team, the two end members of the defense try to dislodge one of the offensive players from the rest of the team. As soon as this is accomplished, the down is over. The ball is put into play from that point. The defensive team returns to the goal line on each play, and the offensive team repeats the same procedure. If no touchdown is scored in four tries, the defense becomes the offense and gets the ball at the 20-yard line going the other direction. All teams must walk while the ball is in play. If the defense breaks its chain, they must reunite before proceeding down the field. If the offensive chain breaks, the down is automatically over. Score the game any way you wish.

KOOKY KICKBALL

This game can be played on either a baseball diamond or on an open field. Like regular kickball (or baseball), one team is up to bat and the other is in the field.

The first batter kicks the ball as it is rolled to him by a teammate. A miss, foul, or ball caught in the air is an out. There are three outs per team per inning. If no outs are made, everyone on the team may go up once during the inning. When the ball is kicked, the fielding team lines up behind the fielder who retrieves the ball. The ball is passed between the legs of all players from front to rear. The last team member then takes the ball and tags the runner.

Meanwhile, the kickers (or batters) do not run around the bases. Instead, the team that is up to bat lines up single file behind the batter, who runs around the team as many times as possible. One run is scored for every complete revolution before the batter is tagged with the ball. Play as many innings as you wish.

LAP SIT

This is one of the best cooperative games. It requires that everyone do a part, or the game flops. It is best with large groups, from fifty to five hundred—even more if you have the room and the people.

Have the group form a large circle with everyone facing clockwise or counterclockwise. Make sure the spacing between each player is about the same. Usually about twelve to eighteen inches is ideal. Then at a signal, everyone holds his arms out to the sides and sits down in the lap of the person immediately behind them. Everyone holds everyone else up. But if one person is out of place, then the whole group will most likely fall down.

The fun of this game is trying to succeed on the first try. But if you aren't successful, try again until the group finally makes it. After you have succeeded, have the group walk while in the seated position. This really takes coordination on everyone's part.

PENGUIN FOOTBALL

Give each person a rag about four inches wide and two feet long (sheets torn into strips work well). Each person then ties the rag securely around his knees to make running impossible. Players can move only by shuffling their feet.

Now divide into teams and play football using a Nerf football. The game becomes hilarious when players must hike, run, throw, and kick with their knees tied together. Of course, this opens up the possibility of playing Penguin Baseball, Penguin Volleyball, Penguin Soccer, and countless other games.

PLUNGERBALL

Here's another great variation of baseball your kids will love. To play, you need a large rubber or plastic ball (not too heavy) and a standard toilet plunger. This game can be played indoors or outdoors.

Divide into two teams. One team is in the field and the other is at bat. The team at bat pokes at the ball with the rubber part on the end of the plunger. The runner runs to first, and all the normal rules of baseball or softball apply.

You can change the rules as you see fit. For example, it's usually best to have four or five bases closer together. Boundaries can be adjusted, and positions in the field can be created spontaneously. Players can be called out by hitting them with the ball. Also, you can have five outs per inning.

POLISH BASEBALL

This is one of the all-time great games for large groups. It sounds ridiculous, but it is exciting and lots of fun to play. It is best when you have teams of about twenty to twenty-five each. You will also need a big open field (you don't need a baseball diamond).

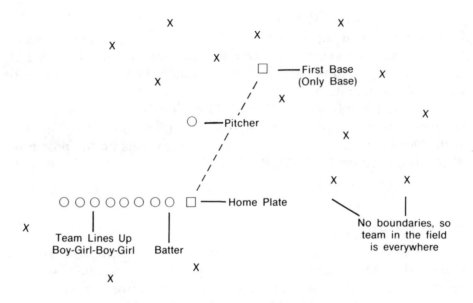

There are only two bases in Polish Baseball—home plate and first base. First base should be about one hundred feet away from home plate (maybe farther away if you have an athletic group). A regular baseball or softball bat is used to hit the ball. The ball is a volleyball with some of the air let out of it, so it won't travel quite so far when hit.

There are no out-of-bounds. The ball can be hit in any direction. In fact, when the ball is pitched, the batter could quickly turn around and hit it behind him if he wanted.

Each inning the team at bat lines up boy-girl-boy-girl on one side of home plate. They go up to bat in that order to give everyone a chance and to insure the batting order is not all "heavy hitters." The team in the field does not play by position, except a catcher at home plate and a first baseman. Everyone else goes wherever he thinks the ball might be hit.

The team at bat provides its own pitcher. The pitch should be as easy as possible to hit. The batter gets one swing at the ball. There are no foul balls. If the bat touches the ball in any way, it's a fair ball. Outs are made in the following ways:

1. A missed swing (a strike is an out)
2. A fly ball that is caught (like in regular baseball)
3. A force out at first base (like in regular baseball)
4. Being tagged with the ball (the runner can be hit with the ball while running to or from first base)

Once a runner reaches first base, he does not have to leave until it is safe, even if the next batter gets a hit. Any number of players can occupy first base at the same time. No runs are scored, however, until players cross home plate. For example, several players on first base might all run to home plate at the same time and score several runs.

There are three outs per inning. As soon as the team at bat has three outs, they run out into the field and take their positions. The team in the field quickly lines up and starts hitting. They don't have to wait for the fielding team to get ready.

If you have more than fifty players, get two games going at once on opposite sides of the field and overlapping each other. It can get very confusing, but it's a lot of fun. Each game will need an umpire to keep score and rule on controversial plays.

POOP DECK

Here's a great game for ten to one hundred. Play in a fairly large room or outside. Clearly mark off three sections on the floor with tape, chalk, etc. One section is the Poop Deck, one the Main Deck, and the last the Quarter Deck. Begin with everyone standing on the Poop Deck. Call the name of a deck (even the one that they are standing in) and the kids then run to the deck that you have called. The last person on the deck is out. If the kids are on Poop Deck, for example, and you call, "Poop Deck," any kid who crosses the line, jumps the gun, or in any other way (except being pushed) goes off the Poop Deck section is out. The game continues until one person is the winner.

POOPDECK	MAINDECK	QUARTERDECK

Other hints on playing this game: Give the kids a few trial runs to warm up and to get the hang of the game; call the decks loudly and distinctly; and occasionally point to the opposite deck you call to confuse them thoroughly.

POWER BASEBALL

Here's a variation of softball that allows a mixed group to have a competitive softball game. Sometimes with a regular softball, some people have a hard time hitting the ball out of the infield and thus are branded "easy outs." So instead of using a softball and bat, use a tennis ball and tennis racquet. Anyone can hit a good shot, and it's almost impossible to strike out. (If some guys hit too far with the new equipment, make them use a racquetball racquet or a regular bat.) This game is especially good for large groups, with fifteen or more people on a side.

RUN THE GAUNTLET

This old game is one of the best outdoor coed games there is. Girls are given rolled-up newspapers and lined up in two single-file lines. The two lines are parallel, facing each other with approximately three to four feet between them. The boys tie balloons to their seats (on their belt loops) and must "run the gauntlet," that is, they must run between the two lines of girls who try to pop the balloons by hitting them with the newspapers. Once a boy's balloon is popped, he is out. This continues until only one boy is left—the winner.

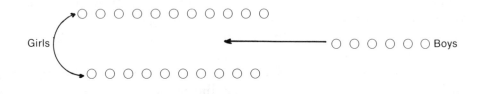

SIAMESE SOFTBALL

This is a good game for a group too large to play a regular softball game. Teams are evenly divided, and team members are paired by hooking their arms together. At no time while playing are they allowed to unhook their arms or use their hooked arms. They may use their free arms and hands. A rubber ball or volleyball is used instead of a softball because it can be caught with the pair's free arms and hands. Only one person needs to throw the ball.

When at bat, pairs are to grasp the bat with their free hands together. After the ball is hit, the pair must run the bases with arms hooked together. Other than these three exceptions, regular softball rules apply.

TAIL-GRAB

Divide the group into any number of equal chains (a line of people in which each person grips the wrist of the one in front of him). The last person in the chain has a tail (a handkerchief) dangling behind. The object is for the first person in the chain to snatch the tail from another line. The fun is to maneuver to get someone else's tail while trying to keep your own.

THREEBALL

Here's a great outdoor game from New Zealand that can be used with almost any age group and any number of people. You need a baseball diamond (or a reasonable facsimile) and three balls of any kind. You can use softballs, footballs, Rugby balls, soccer balls, volleyballs, or just about anything that can be thrown, such as Frisbees. The three balls you use don't have to be the same. You will also need a cardboard box, trash can, bucket, or something that the balls can go in.

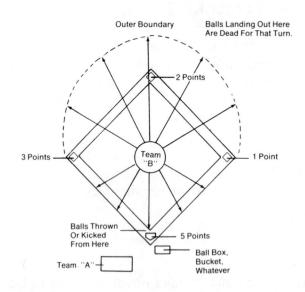

The ball box goes at home plate. One team is at bat, and the other team is out in the field, just like regular baseball. Everybody plays everywhere. The first batter comes to the plate and selects three balls (if there are more than three to choose from). He then must get rid of all three of them as quickly as possible, any way he wants—by kicking, throwing, etc. The balls must stay within the boundaries of the field.

After getting rid of the balls, he starts running the bases while the team in the field tries to return all three balls to the box. The runner gets a point for each base he reaches before the balls are back and five points if he gets a home run (makes it all the way around). If a ball is caught on the fly, then that ball is dead (does not have to be placed). If the runner is caught between bases when the last of the three balls are placed in the box, then he loses all his accumulated points. He must watch and stop safely on a base when all the balls are finally in.

There are no outs. The best way to play is to let everyone on the team have a chance each inning and add up the total points scored. When everybody has batted, then the other team is at bat and tries to get as many points as possible. You can play as many innings as you want. If you have larger groups, then get several games going at once. It doesn't matter if the fields overlap.

Since it is very easy to get to first base (at least), everyone can contribute to the team score and have fun. You will need one referee to blow the whistle (or whatever) when the balls come in and to help keep score. Boundaries, distance between bases, etc. can all be adjusted depending on the size and skill of the group.

TUBE MANIA

Here's a physically exhausting game that can be lots of fun but might be best if played boys against boys and girls against girls.

Mark a large square in the field and place a stack of seven to ten inner tubes in the center of the square. Divide the group into four equal teams, each one lining up on one side of the square. Number the players on each team.

The object of the game is to get as many inner tubes as possible across your team's line. Call several numbers. The players with those numbers run to the center and start dragging the inner tubes to their lines. There may be several players tugging on the same tube. Each tube successfully pulled across a team's line scores points for that team.

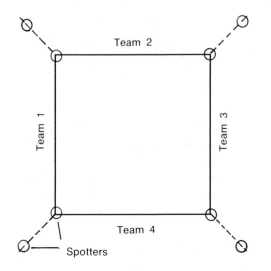

Once the kids get the hang of it, add a soccer ball to the game. Each team gets points deducted from the score if the ball is kicked over the team's line. Team members along the line act as goalies. Once the ball touches the ground in their territory, points are scored against them.

To further complicate the game, add a cage ball (four to eight feet in diameter). The team that gets this ball across their own line gets triple points.

TUG OF WAR

An old-fashioned tug of war never fails to be a winner. Just get a thick, long rope and put one team on each end of it. Whichever team can pull the other one across the line or into a nice, big mud hole in the middle is the winner. For laughs, put grease all over the rope and see what happens.

TUG OF WAR TIMES TWO

By tying two ropes in the middle, so you have four ends of equal length, you can have a tug of war with four teams instead of two. Draw a circle on the ground so that each team is outside the circle when the war begins.

When one team is pulled across the circle line, it is eliminated from the game, leaving the other three teams to tug against each other. Then those three play until another is eliminated, and finally two teams play to determine the winner. Each time, the tug of war is conducted across the circle.

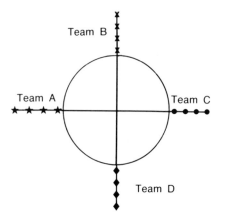

For a TUG OF WAR TIMES THREE, get three ropes and begin with six teams. It works! The primary advantage to this version of tug of war is that the least strong teams can gang up on the strongest teams and eliminate them from the game early.

VOLLEY TENNIS

Volley tennis is played on a tennis court with a volleyball. It is a great game for as many as want to play and requires no great athletic ability. The serve is just like regular volleyball, from behind the back line. But the receiving team must allow the ball to hit the court before touching the ball. They have up to three volleys to get the ball back across the net, but the ball must touch the court between each volley. The game is played to fifteen points, and only the serving team can score. Line hits are in play. This is most fun when at least a dozen people are on each team.

3.

OUTDOOR GAMES
FOR
SMALL GROUPS

All of the games in this chapter are ideal for small groups of thirty or less in an outdoor setting. They can, of course, be played with larger groups as well, often with little or no adapting required.

Many of the games in chapters 2, 4, and 5 can also be adapted for small group use outdoors. See especially chapter 7.

BADMINTON VOLLEYBALL

Here is a crazy version of volleyball that works well with groups from six to forty. Have each person bring a badminton racquet to the game. In case there are those who do not have badminton racquets, you might have to provide a few extra. Even if you have to buy them, they are usually not very expensive. You'll also need a couple of birdies (shuttlecocks). Divide into two teams and play badminton over a volleyball net, using regular volleyball rules. This can really be a riot with fifteen to twenty kids on each side of the net. For mixed groups, you might have all the guys play wrong-handed.

BOOK VOLLEYBALL

Here's another adaptation of volleyball. It's just like regular volleyball with two exceptions. First, everyone must use a book (any size) instead of his hands to hit the ball. Obviously, it is best to use a hardbound book. Second, a tennis ball or Nerf ball is used instead of a volleyball. The rest of the usual volleyball rules apply.

BROOM HOCKEY

This game can be played with as many as thirty or as few as five per team, but only five or six are actually on the field at one time from each team. Two teams compete (at a whistle) by running onto the field, grabbing their brooms, and swatting a volleyball, placed in the center, through the opposite goal. Each team has a goalie, like in ice hockey or soccer, who can grab the ball with his hands and throw it back onto the playing field. If the ball goes out-of-bounds, a referee throws it back in. The ball cannot be touched with hands or feet, only with brooms. Score one point for each time the ball passes between goal markers.

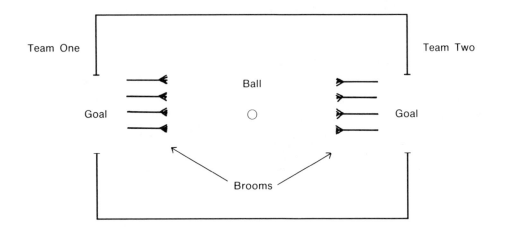

For a team with thirty members, for example, have them number off by sixes, which would give you six teams of five members each. Let all the ones play a three minute period, then the twos, etc.

BUCKET BRIGADE

For this game, you need two teams. Each team lines up single file with a bucket of water on one end and an empty bucket on the other. Each team member has a paper cup. The object of the game is to transfer the water from one bucket to the other by pouring the water from cup to cup down the line. The first team to get all of the water to the empty bucket is the winner.

43

CENTIPEDE RACE

Here's a great game that can be played indoors or outdoors. All you need are some benches. Seat as many kids on each bench as possible, straddling it like a horse. When the race starts, everyone must stand up, bend over, and pick up the bench, holding it between his legs. They then run like a centipede. The finish line should be forty to fifty feet away. It's a lot of fun to watch.

CHINESE VOLLEYBALL

This game is played just like Chinese Ping-Pong (page 109), where everyone stands around a Ping-Pong table and rotates around the table. The only difference is instead of using a Ping-Pong table, use a volleyball court and a volleyball. The ball can bounce once before being hit, just like regular Ping-Pong. This game can also be played on a tennis court using tennis balls and tennis racquets.

CIRCLE SOCCER

Two teams get into one circle, half on one side and half on the other.

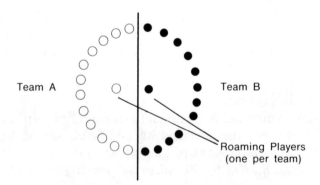

A ball is thrown into the circle, and the players try to kick it out through the other team's side. If the ball is kicked out over the heads of the players, the point goes to the nonkicking team. If the ball is kicked out below the heads of the players, the kicking team gets the point. Hands may not be used at all, only feet and bodies.

No one may move out of position except one player per team who may kick the ball to his teammates if the ball gets stuck in the center. He may not score, however, or cross into the other team's territory. If the roaming player gets hit with the ball (when kicked by the other team), the kicking team gets a point.

CRAZY SOCCER

Here's another exciting version of soccer. In many respects, it's just like ordinary soccer, except that you use four goals instead of two, with four teams at the same time, each defending a goal.

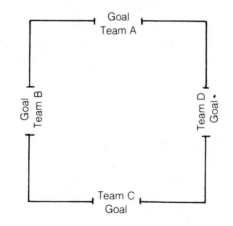

With this configuration, you can have two soccer games going at once (one going each way); you can combine teams, so teams A and C play teams B and D. Each combined team must then defend two goals. You can use one or two balls.

CRAZY VOLLEYBALL

If you don't have quite enough kids to get a "real" volleyball game going or if you have several inept players, here's a fun version of the game with a few new rules:

1. Each team may hit the ball four times before hitting it over the net.
2. A ball hitting the floor counts as one hit.

These rules keep the ball in play over a much longer period of time.

CROQUET-GOLF

This is actually miniature golf played with a croquet set. The wickets are used instead of cups in the ground. Set up your own nine hole course by arranging the wickets around the yard. Tag each wicket with the hole number as well as placing small signs at each tee where the players must begin each hole. Determine how many strokes will be par for each hole and indicate this on the tee sign along with the hole number. Try to make each hole different by having to go around objects such as shrubs, through tin cans and tires, and up ramps and hills. Some croquet sets include wicket tags and tee signs for playing Croquet-Golf.

CROWS AND CRANES

Divide the group into two teams. One side is the Crows; the other the Cranes. The two teams are lined up facing each other four or five feet apart. The leader flips a coin (heads—Crows, tails—Cranes) and shouts the name of the team that won the toss. If he yells, "Crows," the Crows must turn around and run, with the Cranes in hot pursuit. If any of the Cranes succeed in touching a member (or members) of the Crows before he crosses a given line (twenty to sixty feet away), he is considered a captive of the Cranes and must aid the Cranes when play continues. The team that captures all the members of the other team is the winner.

FLAMINGO FOOTBALL

Announce that you are going to play "tackle football, boys against the girls!" The guys usually get pretty charged up about that idea. Then announce that the rules are the same as regular tackle football, except the boys must hold one foot off the ground with one hand at all times. They must run, pass, hike, catch, and even kick on one foot. The girls usually clobber the guys in this game.

FRISBASKETBALL

Next time your group wants to play basketball, why not try this one? Instead of a basketball, use a Frisbee and as many players as you wish on a regular basketball court. Of course, you can't dribble a Frisbee, so you must advance it by passing. The refs should call penalties such as fouls, travelling, and out-of-bounds just as they normally would in a basketball game. Points should be awarded as follows: one point for hitting the backboard, two for hitting the square on the backboard, and three for making a goal (including foul shots). Double the scores for any shot made from behind midcourt.

FRISBEE ATTACK

Here's an exciting new version of Frisbee Tag. To play, you'll need a playing area with a radius of about forty feet. The game is best played with five to ten players. One person is chosen to be IT; another to be the Frisbee Thrower. IT is free to move around, while the Frisbee Thrower must stand in the middle of the bounded area, preferably on a chair or table. You will also need at least three Frisbees (or other flying discs).

The object of the game is for IT to get the other players out by hitting them with a Frisbee. As the game begins, IT has all the Frisbees and tries to hit the other players with them. If hit, the player is frozen and can no longer move. If IT misses, the Frisbee can be captured by anyone who wants to run after it. When a Frisbee is captured, the player who has it can try to get it to the Frisbee Thrower in the middle of the field, either by carrying it or throwing it. This is important because only the Frisbee Thrower is able to unfreeze players by throwing a Frisbee to one of the frozen players who must catch it before it hits the ground. In catching the Frisbee, the frozen player may only move one foot. If both feet are used, the throw is invalid. If unfrozen, the player may give the Frisbee back to the Frisbee Thrower to release another frozen player.

Meanwhile, IT is still scrambling around trying to hit players with Frisbees, intercept captured Frisbees, and so on. The game ends when IT has frozen everyone and the Frisbee Thrower has no more Frisbees to throw. As more players are added, more ITS can also be added. Find the right balance to keep the competition even.

Allow everyone a chance to be IT and give a prize to the one who can freeze everyone in the shortest time. You might want to set a time limit for each IT.

FRISBEE GOLF

Lay out a short golf course around the area using telephone poles, light posts, fence posts, tree trunks, etc. for holes. You can set up places as the tees or designate a certain distance from the previous hole (perhaps ten feet) for the starting place. Each person needs a Frisbee. The object of the game is to take as few throws as possible to hit all the holes. Each person takes a throw from the tee and then stands where it landed for the next throw until he hits the hole. Of course, discretion must be used when the Frisbee lands in a bush or tree. One penalty throw is added to the score if the Frisbee can't be thrown from where it lands. The course can be as simple or as complicated as the skill of the participants warrants. Such things as doglegs, doorways, arches, and narrow fairways add to the fun of the course. Take three or four good Frisbee throwers through the course to set the par for each hole. It is a good test of skill, but anybody can do it.

FRISBEE SOCCER

Play a regular game of soccer, only use a Frisbee instead of a soccer ball. Players must move the Frisbee (the ball) by tossing it from one player to another. You cannot run with the Frisbee. Other rules of soccer apply. Goals should be cages that will catch the Frisbee when the goal is made. You could also use a hoop (or tire) that the Frisbee must pass through to score a goal. In that case, no goalies are allowed.

Another version of this game is to have a Frisbee free-for-all where a dozen or two Frisbees are placed in the center of the playing area. When the game starts, players try to get as many Frisbees as possible into their goal. Once a Frisbee is in the goal, it stays there. Again, they may only be passed. It's really a wild game.

HAT AND GO SEEK

Here's a game that combines the best of tag and hide-and-go-seek. One person wears an old hat, hides his eyes, and gives the rest of the group one minute to run and hide. Then, the hat-wearer begins to search. (The hat must be worn, not carried.)

When someone is found and tagged, that person must wear the hat, cover his eyes for twenty counts, and continue the search. Each person should keep track of how many times he wears the hat. The one who wears it the least number of times wins.

HUMAN FOOSBALL

Many churches and recreation centers have a Foosball table, which is a table version of soccer. Using an open field, the Foosball format may be reconstructed making for a wild and fast game of soccer.

Begin by dividing a playing field into ten sections. You may divide the field by using lime on the ground, or an even better method is to use string or cord strung across the field about waist high. (You may run the string across the field and attach it at both ends to folding chairs.)

Once the field is divided, then it is time to arrange the players. Each team should use an equal number of players; normally ten is about right, but you may want to adjust that number depending on field size and the number of people who want to participate. Arrange the players in the sections as shown in the following diagram. The players on the outer edges of the field are called spotters.

Once set up, the game itself is simple. The object of the game is to kick the ball into the other team's goal. The ball may be advanced using any part of the body, except the hands and arms. Unlike normal soccer, this rule also applies to the goalie who is stationed in the first section away from the goal. Players may only advance the ball while it is in their sections and may move laterally as much as they like, but they may not break the plane that serves as the boundaries for their section.

To enforce this rule, players who range out of their section are removed from the game for two minutes along with everyone else who is in that section with him. It is the job of the spotters to roll the ball back into play once it has been kicked out-of-bounds. As shown in the diagram, the spotters are placed around the field alternately to keep the game fair. The number of spotters used will depend upon the number of participants.

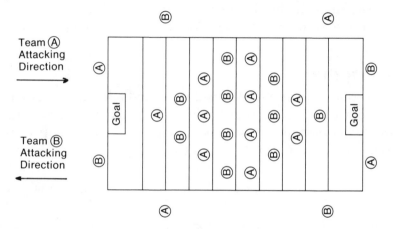

Here are a few helpful hints to keep the game moving: Be sure the spotters throw the ball back as soon as they retrieve it; develop a rotation system so that everyone can play the different positions; and finally, use any round ball, but normally a little heavier ball, such as a regulation soccer ball, works best.

INNER-TUBE SOCCER

This is a game of soccer that uses the usual rules of the game only substitutes an inner tube (automobile tire tube) for the soccer ball. It really gives the game a new dimension. The tube should lie flat, and the playing surface should be relatively flat and smooth.

JUNGLE FOOTBALL

This is essentially touch or flag football. However, all players are eligible to catch a pass. The quarterback (ball carrier) can also run across the line of scrimmage and still pass the ball forward, backward, etc. to another player. Multiple passes are allowed (several passes on one play). Each team gets four downs to score. There aren't any first downs. Only touchdowns are counted (six points) and safeties (two points). The rules can be changed or modified to fit any size group, age, sex, etc. Have your own Jungle Football Super Bowl!

LINE SOCCER

Here's a variation of soccer that is simple and a lot of fun. Divide your group into two equal teams. Each team numbers off and lines up opposite each other about thirty feet apart. (A gym floor will work fine.) A line can be drawn in front of each team to designate the scoring area.

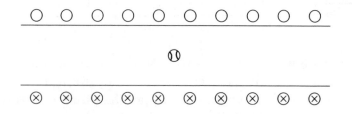

A ball is placed in the middle of the field, and a referee calls a number. The players on each team with that number run to the ball and try to kick it through the opposite team (across their line). It must go between them, below the heads (or below the waist) to count as a goal. The defenders can catch the ball and toss it back to their own player or kick it back when it comes to them. After a minute or two, the referee calls a new number. It really gets wild when you call several numbers at once.

A good variation of this game is to play the game with four teams. The four lines are laid out as a square. When a number is called, four players (one from each team) run to the center and try to kick the ball through any one of the other three teams. It's really a wild game.

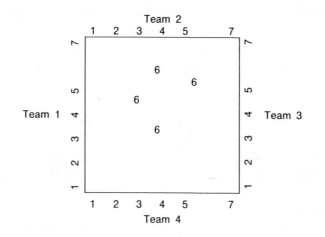

MONKEY SOCCER

Yet another way to make your next soccer game even more challenging is to have players play any version of soccer using their hands (fists) to advance the ball, rather than their feet. Players must move in a squatting position, so their hands almost touch the floor.

NEW VOLLEYBALL

Here is a great new way to play the old game of volleyball. New Volleyball can be played on a regular volleyball court with the normal amount of players on each team. A regular volleyball is used as well. The main difference is the scoring.

The object of the game is for a team to volley the ball as many times as possible without missing or fouling (up to fifty times) before hitting it back over the net to the opposing team who will make every attempt to return it without missing. If they do miss, the opposite team receives as many points as they volleyed before returning it. All volleys must be counted audibly by the entire team (or by scorers on the sidelines), which aids in the scoring process and also helps build tension. So the idea is to volley the ball as many times as possible each time the ball comes over the net, then to safely return it, and to hope that the other team blows it.

Other rules are as follows:

1. No person may hit the ball two consecutive times.
2. No two people may hit the ball back and forth to each other more than once in succession to increase the number of volleys. In other words, Player A may hit it to player B, but Player B may not hit it back to Player A. Player A may hit it again once someone else has hit it besides Player B.
3. Five points are awarded to the serving team if the opposing team fails to return a serve.
4. Five points are awarded to the receiving team if a serve is missed (out-of-bounds, in the net, etc.).
5. Players rotate on each serve, even if the serving team scores on successive serves.
6. A game is fifteen minutes. The highest score wins.
7. All other volleyball rules are in effect.

OVER THE LINE

Here's a great softball game that has become very popular on Southern California beaches in recent years. All that is needed is a bat and a softball, six people (three on a team) and some way to mark the boundaries of the playing field (see the following diagram).

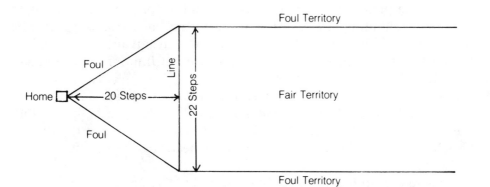

The batter on the team at bat stands at home plate and tries to hit the ball over the line (in the air) in fair territory. The ball is pitched from someone on the team at bat in one of two ways: (A) the official way (the way it is normally pitched, although sometimes dangerous) is for the pitcher to kneel beside the batter and toss the ball straight up for the batter to hit.

(B) The pitch may also be delivered in the conventional way with the pitcher standing fifteen or twenty feet from the batter (anywhere he wants) and lobbing the ball up to be hit. The disadvantage is that it is harder to get a hit this way. The pitcher cannot interfere with the ball after it is hit or the batter is out.

The team in the field positions themselves in fair territory (anywhere they want). If they catch a hit ball before it hits the ground, the batter is out. Anything that drops into fair territory on the fly is a base hit. A ball hit in fair territory over the heads of all three fielders is a home run.

There are no bases, so no base running. The bases are imaginary. When a person gets a base hit, the next batter comes up and hits. It takes three base hits (not four as in regular softball) before a run is scored, then every base hit after that adds another run. A home run after the first three base hits would score four runs (clearing the bases, plus one bonus run), and it takes three more base hits to start scoring runs again. Other rules include these:

1. Each batter gets only two pitches to get a hit (only one foul, mis-swing, etc.). If you don't get a hit in two pitches, you are out.
2. Any ball hit on the ground in front of the line is an out. (Unless it's foul on the first pitch.)
3. Each team gets three outs per inning, as in regular softball.
4. The game is played for nine innings (or as many as you want).

Of course, the rules of the game can be modified as you wish. For example, the boundaries can be adjusted to fit the skills of the players. Or instead of using a softball, you could use a mush ball or a volleyball. You could play with more (or less) on a team. It is great on the beach as well as on a regular playing field. Be creative and have fun.

OVER THE LINE II

Here's a slightly more complicated version of the previous game. The playing field, the three-person teams, and the other rules remain pretty much the same with a few modifications. For example, the field has two more lines (see the diagram below).

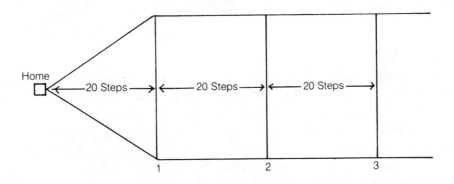

If the batter hits the ball between lines 1 and 2, it goes as a single. Between lines 2 and 3 is a double. Over line 3 is a triple, and over the head of the last opposing player is a home run. The defending players can play anywhere in the field, but usually it is best to have one player defending each of the three territories.

The scoring is exactly like regular baseball, but all runs must be forced home. For instance, if there is a man on first and second, (base runners are still imaginary—nobody really runs) and the next batter hits a double, then one run scores and now there are men on second and third. If the next player hits a single, nobody scores (first base is open). Another single would score a run (the bases were loaded).

Singles, doubles, and triples are usually only counted as such when the ball crosses the appropriate line in the air. However for more excitement and larger scores, it can be done this way: A single must land behind line 1 on the fly (as usual), but a single can also be scored if a "grounder" is hit and it rolls across the first line without being stopped. Similarly, if the fielder lets the ball roll or bounce past line 2 in fair territory, then it is a double, even though it hit the ground in single territory. Same thing with a triple. If the ball crosses the third line, no matter how it got there, it goes as a triple. Home runs are still the same (over everyone's head). All other rules are the same as regular Over the Line.

ROOFBALL

For this game, you need a volleyball and a roof. Experimentation will tell which roofs are the best. Roofball is unique because each roof produces a new challenge, a different twist to the game.

Decide on the out-of-bounds, form a single file line perpendicular to the line of the roof. The first person in line serves the ball up on the roof and moves to the back of the line. The second person in line must play the ball by hitting the ball (volleyball-style) back onto the roof before it hits the ground. He then moves to the back of the line, and the third player plays the ball. This continues until a miss or a played ball lands out-of-bounds. Three missed balls and a player sits out.

Missed balls are those that don't make it to the roof, hit under the roofline, go over the roof, are completely missed, or land out-of-bounds. Obviously, the player who is responsible for the ball going out is charged with the miss. When you miss, you are out of the game, and the game continues until there is just one person left who is the winner. To play with teams, form one line for each team. The first player on team one hits the ball up onto the roof, and the first player on team two hits it up again, then back to the second person on team one, and so on. Every time somebody misses, the other team gets points.

SARDINES

This game is actually hide-and-seek in reverse. The group chooses one person to be IT. This person hides while the rest of the group counts to one hundred (or a signal is given). Now the group sets out to find the hidden person. Each person should look individually, but small groups (two or three) may look together. When a person finds IT, he hides with IT instead of telling the rest of the group. The hiding place may be changed an unlimited number of times during any game. The last person to find the hidden group, which has now come to resemble a group of sardines, is the loser or IT for the next game.

SCAT

Here's an old game that is probably new for most of your kids. To play, you need a volleyball or playground ball. Everyone is assigned a number with two mystery numbers not assigned to anyone. No one knows what the mystery numbers are except the leader. The person who has the ball throws it up in the air and calls a number. Everyone scatters except the person whose number was called. That person immediately retrieves the ball and yells, "Stop," then tries to hit someone with the ball. If hit, the player gets a letter (S, C, A or T), but if missed, the thrower gets a letter. If a mystery number (chosen by the leader) is called, then everyone automatically gets a letter. The two mystery numbers may be called only once. People who get the four letters S-C-A-T are eliminated.

SHOE KICK

For this simple game, have your guys take off one shoe and hang it off the end of their foot. The idea is to see who can kick his shoe the farthest. You will be surprised to see how many kids kick them over their heads, behind them, or straight up in the air.

SOLO SOCCER

Here's a version of soccer that should appeal to all the rugged individualists in your group. Arrange the players in a large circle with a little space between them. Mark a goal near each player by putting two stakes in the ground about six feet apart. The object is to protect your own goal while trying to score through someone else's. The last person to touch the ball before it goes through the goal receives one point. The person who is scored upon receives a negative point. Goals should not be allowed that are kicked above the goalie's head.

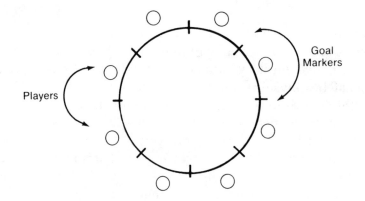

STEAL THE BACON

This is an old favorite, which most groups love to play. Divide into two teams and line up the teams facing each other behind two lines (twenty to thirty feet apart). Each team should number off, so they have the same numbered players, but in opposite directions (see diagram). A handkerchief or towel is placed in the center, at a point equidistant from both teams.

The leader calls a number. The player on each team having that number runs to the center and tries to snatch the handkerchief and return to his goal without being tagged by the other player. The more skilled players will run into the center and hover over the handkerchief until he can snatch it and run when his opponent is off guard. Each successful return gains one point for the team. After each successful tag or score, the handkerchief is returned to the center, and another number is called. Play for a designated number of points. The leader should call numbers in a way that builds suspense. All numbers should be included, but it is well to repeat a number now and then to keep all players alert. Also, maintain interest by calling two or more numbers simultaneously (involving four or more players).

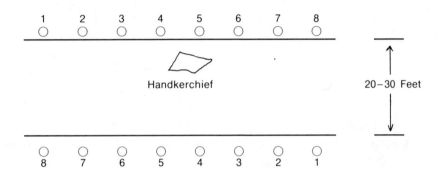

STEAL THE BACON IN-THE-ROUND

Draw a large circle with lines for line-up on opposite sides of the circle. Locate the center. (Circle diameter is approximately fifteen feet. Lime works well in the field or paint on blacktop.) By curving the line-up line, all the kids can see the activity without interfering with the action of the game.

Place the "bacon" (an old shirt, a sponge, or small ball) in the center. The players line up. The first person on each team, at the whistle, runs to the center and tries to grab and carry the bacon over the circle score line. If the person with the bacon is tagged, then the tagging person receives the point. If, after a predetermined time (thirty seconds), neither player picks up the bacon, blow the whistle, and the

61

next two players may join the two in the circle. When two team members are working together, they may pass the bacon between themselves.

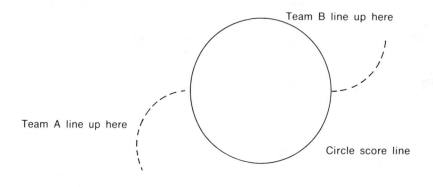

Team B line up here

Team A line up here

Circle score line

Advantages:
1. The circle allows for a person to run in any direction to score.
2. The teams do not have to be equal, in fact, it is better if they are not equal, so the players never compete against the same people on future turns.
3. You do not have to number off players or call numbers.

THROUGH THE LEGS SHUFFLE
Here's the old through-the-legs game with a new twist. Have the teams line up single file spreading their legs apart enough, so someone can crawl through them. Everyone must have his hands on the hips of the person in front. The lines must be behind the starting line. At the signal, the last person crawls through the legs of the team and stands up at the front of the line. As soon as he stands up, the person who is now at the rear of the line crawls through, and so forth. The line moves forward, and the first team to cross the goal line wins. Only one person per team can be crawling at a time.

TUG OF WAR IN THE ROUND

Get a large rope about twenty-four feet in length and tie (or splice) the two ends together, making one round rope. Four teams line up on four sides of a square. In the center of the square, the rope is placed opened out into a circle. The teams should be equal in size, and each team should number off. The leader then calls a number, and the four kids (one from each team) with that number grab one side of the rope and try to get back across their team's line. As soon as a player crosses the line (pulling the rope), he is declared the winner. Continue until everyone has had a try.

UNDERDOG

This is a variation of the old game of tag. Choose one player to be IT. All the players must stay within a given boundary, and IT tries to tag as many free players as possible. When a player is tagged by IT, that player must freeze. Frozen players can be unfrozen (freed) by spreading their legs and allowing another free player to pass between their open legs. IT tries to freeze as many players as possible within a given time limit. You can build excitement by making more than one player IT.

WHIFFLE GOLF

Here's a crazy version of golf, which kids will enjoy. Set up your own golf course on an open field, all over a campground, around houses— just about anywhere. Each hole is a small tin can or jar just big enough for a whiffle ball. The cans can be placed on the ground and anchored there or elevated on poles. After the course is set, each player tees off for hole number one (there can be nine or eighteen holes). No clubs are used. You simply toss the ball underhanded. Each toss counts as a stroke. The idea is to get the ball into the can in the fewest possible strokes. In mixed groups, the girls can toss overhand or any way they want. It is best to play in foursomes, just like regular golf, to set a par for each hole, to print scorecards, etc. You can have a Whiffle Golf Tournament, just like the pros. If you can't get whiffle balls, you can substitute bean-bags.

4.

INDOOR GAMES
FOR
LARGE GROUPS

The games in this chapter are best played indoors with groups of thirty or more. Since most of them require quite a bit of space, play them in a gymnasium, fellowship hall, or recreation room.

Many of these games are easily played outdoors and can be played with smaller groups as well as larger groups. Don't forget there are more games that can be played indoors with large groups in chapter 6, chapter 7, and in several other chapters as well.

ANATOMY SHUFFLE

This game is a variation of BIRDIE ON THE PERCH (page 71). The group pairs off and forms two circles, one inside the other. One member of each couple is on the inside circle; the other in the outside circle.

The outer circle begins traveling in one direction (clockwise), and the inner circle goes in the opposite direction (counterclockwise). The leader blows a whistle and shouts something like "Hand, Ear!" The first body part called is always the inner group's, and they must find their partners, who stand in one position (they cannot move after the whistle blows) and touch their (first body part called) to the (second body part called) on their partners. For example, with "Hand, ear!" the inner circle group must find their partners and place their hand on their partners' ear. The last couple to get the proper position is eliminated each time, and the last couple to remain in the game wins. The leader calls all sorts of combinations, such as these:

"Finger, Foot"	"Nose, Shoulder"
"Thigh, Thigh"	"Head, Stomach"
"Elbow, Nose"	"Nose, Armpit"

BALLOON BASKETBALL

Arrange your chairs in the following manner. There should be the same number of people on each of the two teams that are playing. One team faces in one direction; the second team the other direction. The two rows of chairs on each end should face inward. There can be any number of players on a team.

After all the players are seated in their team's chairs, toss a balloon into the center of the players. The players cannot stand, but they must try to bat the balloon to the end zone that they are facing with their hands. As soon as the balloon drops into the end zone over the heads of the last row of people, the team going that direction wins 2 points (like in basketball). If the balloon goes out-of-bounds, throw it back into the center. Play can continue to twenty points or may end after fifteen minutes.

BALLOON SMASH

Give everyone a balloon and a piece of string. The balloon is blown up and tied around the waist, so it hangs behind the player's back. Each player also makes a "balloon smasher" out of rolled-up newspaper and masking tape. The object is to smash other players' balloons by hitting them with your balloon smasher while protecting your own balloon by moving around as quickly as possible. Once a player's balloon is smashed, he is out of the game. The last player(s) to remain in the game wins.

BALLOON STOMP

This game is similar to the preceding one; however, it is a little easier on the backside. Balloons are tied around each player's ankles with a piece of string. The string should be about ten inches long (between the ankle and the balloon). When the game begins, players try to stomp and pop everyone else's balloons while trying to keep his from being stomped. The last person with a balloon is the winner.

BANANA RACE

This is a good indoor game that requires very little space. Divide a group into four equal teams and arrange chairs in a square (each team being one side of the square). There is a chair in the center, but no one sits in it. The first player at the left end of each team is given a banana. At the signal, the first player runs around the center chair without touching it and back to the right end of his own line. In the meantime, all of his team members have moved up one seat toward the head of the line leaving a vacant chair at the right end. After taking the vacant chair, the first player passes the banana along the line. When the end player receives it, he runs around the center chair and back to the vacant chair. This continues with each player doing this. Each team attempts to be the first to have all players back in their original position. The original first player must eat the banana when his team is finished, and his team wins.

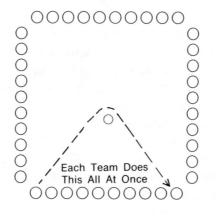

BARNYARD

Give each person a folded piece of paper with the name of an animal written on it. The person is not to say a word or look at the paper. He is to sit down and wait for further instructions. (To insure equal teams assign the same animal to every sixth person.) After everyone is seated, the group is told to look at their team name (the animal), and when the lights are turned out, they are to stand immediately and make the sound of their animals, such as these:

Pig	Chicken
Horse	Duck
Cow	Dog

As soon as they find someone else who is making the same noise, they lock arms and try to find their teammates. When the lights come back on, everyone sits down. The team *most together* wins. For added fun, give one guy in the crowd the word "donkey" on his slip of paper. He'll wander around looking for more donkeys without any luck at all.

BERSERK

Here is a unique game that requires little skill, includes any amount of people, and is 100% active. The object is for a group of any size to keep an equal amount of assigned tennis balls moving about a gymnasium floor until six penalties have been indicated.

The following vocabulary for this game is unique and essential to the success of the game.

RABID NUGGET: a moving tennis ball.

HECTIC: a stationary tennis ball.

BERSERK: a referee's scream, designating a penalty.

FRENZY: an elapsed time period measuring six Berserks.

LOGIC: a tennis ball that becomes lodged unintentionally on or behind something.

ILLOGIC: a tennis ball that is craftily stuck on or behind something.

PARANOIA: a player's feeling that the refs are picking on him.

If thirty players are on the gym floor, thirty Rabid Nuggets are thrown, rolled, or bounced simultaneously onto the floor by one of the refs. There are three refs—one at each end of the court and one at midcourt. It is the duty of the two refs on the floor to try and spot Hectics and to generate a hysterical scream (a Berserk), so all will recognize a penalty. The group has five seconds to start a Hectic moving again or another full-throated Berserk is issued. The Berserking ref must point condemningly at the Hectic until it is again given impetus.

Every fifteen seconds after a start, the midcourt ref puts an additional Rabid Nugget into play until the final Berserk has been recorded.

The team is allowed six Berserks, then the midcourt ref, who is responsible for timing this melee, jumps up and down waving his arms and yelling, "STOP. . . .STOP. . . .STOP."

The object is to keep the Rabid Nuggets moving as long as possible before the Frenzy is called. After a Frenzy, ask the group to develop a strategy to keep the Rabid Nuggets moving for a longer Frenzy.

Other rules include these:
1. A Rabid Nugget must be kicked (only kicked) randomly or to another player. It must not be held underfoot and simply moved back and forth.
2. If a Rabid Nugget becomes a Logic or Illogic, the ref must get the nugget back into motion. An Illogic receives an immediate Berserk.

BIRDIE ON THE PERCH

Have kids pair off and get into two concentric circles. If they are boy-girl couples, then the boys should be in the outside circle, and the girls should be in the inside circle.

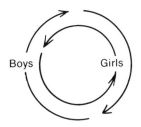

At the whistle, the boys' circle begins moving clockwise and the girls' circle moves counterclockwise. When the leader yells, "Birdie on the Perch!", the boys stop where they are and get down on one knee.

The girls must quickly locate their partner and sit on his extended knee and put her arms around his neck. The last couple to get into that position is eliminated. The game continues until only one couple remains.

BIRTHDAY BARNYARD

This game is an adaptation of Barnyard (page 69). Give each person a list like the one below. After everyone has received the list, the players are instructed to look at the action described for the month of their birthday. When the lights are turned out, they are to stand up immediately and make the appropriate action. As soon as they find a person doing the same thing, they lock arms and look for the rest of the team. As soon as all the team is together, they are to sit down. The first team to find all its members wins.

> January—Shout "Happy New Year!"
> February—Say "Be My Valentine"
> March—Blow (wind)
> April—Hop (Easter Bunny)
> May—say "Mother, May I?"
> June—say "Will you marry me?"
> July—Make fireworks sounds
> August—Sing "Take me out to the ball game"
> September—Fall down (fall) repeatedly
> October—shout "Boo!"
> November—say "Gobble-Gobble"
> December—say "Ho Ho Ho, Merrrry Christmas"

BIRTHDAY RACES

Divide into teams of equal size. On "go," each team must line up according to their date of birth, with the youngest person on one end of the line and the oldest on the other. Round two can be by birthdate (regardless of age), with January 1st (the first birthdate in the calendar year) on one end of the line and December 31st (the last birthday in the year) on the other.

BLIND SARDINES

Here's a good noncompetitive game for large groups. You will need a blindfold for everyone. To play, one person is appointed (or volunteers) to be the sardine. The sardine may or may not wear a blindfold (your choice). All the other players wear blindfolds, and their objective is to come into contact with the sardine. As the players mill around the floor, when one player touches or bumps into another, he grabs the other player and asks, "Are you the sardine?" The sardine must answer, "Yes" if asked. Once a person finds the sardine, he must hang onto the sardine for the remainder of the game and becomes a sardine. Eventually more and more players are bumping into the line of sardines and adding themselves to the chain. The game is over when everyone has become part of the sardine chain.

BROOM SOCCER

Arrange chairs in an oval, open at both ends. An equal number of kids sit on both sides. Each kid has a number, with the same numbers on each team. In other words, there would be a number one player on each team, a number two on each team, and so on. To begin, the number ones come to the center, and each is given a broom. A rubber or plastic ball is tossed into the middle, and the game begins. The two players try to knock the ball with the brooms through the opponent's goal. Each team is assigned one of the two open ends of the oval as their goal. The referee can shout a new number anytime, and the two players in the center must drop the brooms where they are, and the two new players grab the brooms and continue. Play continues as long as the ball is in the oval. If it is knocked out, the referee returns it into play. Players in the chairs cannot touch the ball with their hands (intentionally) but may kick it if it is hit at their feet.

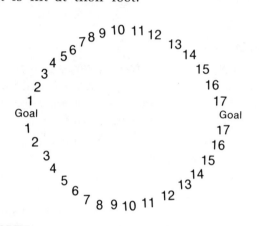

CATASTROPHE

This game can be used with a group of twenty-four or more people. Divide the group into three teams and have each team sit in chairs in three lines that are parallel with about three feet between the teams. All players should be facing the same direction toward the front of their team's line. (Each player sits facing a teammate's back.)

Each team has the name of a town, such as, "Pottstown," "Mudsville," and "Dry Gulch" (any name will do). Each player on each team is assigned an occupation, such as plumber, carpenter, policeman, preacher, teacher, doctor, etc. There should be the same occupations on each team, and they should be seated in the same order on each team as well.

The leader then calls an occupation and a town, such as, "We need a policeman at Pottstown." At that point, the policemen on each team must get up out of their chairs, run around their team, and return to their chairs. The first person back in his chair wins a point for his team.

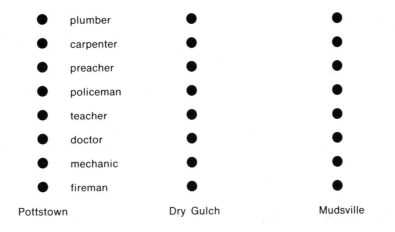

	Pottstown	Dry Gulch	Mudsville
●	plumber	●	●
●	carpenter	●	●
●	preacher	●	●
●	policeman	●	●
●	teacher	●	●
●	doctor	●	●
●	mechanic	●	●
●	fireman	●	●

An additional twist to this game is that players must run around their teams in the right direction. This is determined by which town is called. For example, if the team lines are arranged so Pottstown is on everyone's left, Mudsville is on the right, and Dry Gulch is in the middle, then if Mudsville is called, everyone must get out of his chair on the right and run around the team in a clockwise (right) direction. Pottstown would be left, and if Dry Gulch is called, either direction is okay. If you don't run in the correct direction, you lose.

If the leader shouts, "There's been a catastrophe in (town)!", then everyone on all three teams must get up and run around his team, again in the correct direction. The first team completely seated is the winner. Remember that everyone must get up from his chair on the correct side, as well as run around in the right direction.

CHAIN TAG

Here is a fast-moving game that can be played both indoors or outdoors. It's a game of tag where one person begins as IT, and his job is to catch people (tag them). When he catches someone, then the two of them join hands and continue catching people as a unit. Once there is eight in the group, it breaks apart and becomes two groups of four. This continues with each group of four trying to catch the remaining people. Every time they catch four more, they break off and form a new group of four. The result is several groups of four chasing the free single players who have not been caught. The game is played until everyone is caught. Running in groups is a lot of fun, and the effect is something like "crack the whip."

CLOTHESPINNING

Here's a wild game that is simple, yet fun to play with any size group. Give everyone in the group six clothespins. On "go," each player tries to pin their clothespins on other players' clothing. Each of your six pins must be hanged on six different players. You must keep moving to avoid having clothespins on you while you try to hang your pins on someone else. When you hang all six of your clothespins, you remain in the game but try to avoid having more pins hanged on you. At the end of a time limit, the person with the least amount of clothespins is the winner, and the person with the most is the loser.

Another way to play this is to divide the group into pairs and give each person six clothespins. Each person then tries to hang all his pins on his partner. When the whistle is blown, the player with the least number of pins on his clothes is the winner. The winners continue to pair off until there is a champion clothespinner.

CLUMPS

This game can be used for as many as one thousand. People crowd to the center with their arms at their sides. They are instructed to keep moving and crowding toward the center. They must keep their arms at their sides. The leader blows a whistle or foghorn to stop all movement and immediately shouts a number. If the number is four, for instance, everyone must get into groups of four, lock arms, and sit down. Referees then eliminate all those not in groups of four. This is repeated, with different numbers each time until all have been eliminated.

A variation of this game is called "Tin Pan Bang Bang." In this game, no number is shouted. Instead, the leader bangs on a stainless steel pot with a big metal spoon. The players must listen and count the number of bangs. If the leader stops banging on the pot after five bangs, then the players must get into groups of five.

You can add a further element to the game by dividing the group into two separate teams. Then, the players mingle around until the leader shouts (or bangs out) a number. At that point, they must get into a group of the designated number but only with members of their own team.

CLUMPS TAG

Here's a great game that combines "tag" with "Clumps." It can be played with any number of people and should be played in a space that has boundaries, like a large room or a basketball court. One person is IT. The leader should have either a PA system or a loud referee's whistle.

The game begins with everyone milling around, including the person who is IT. As soon as the whistle is blown, IT may begin to tag people. The referee blows the whistle a certain number of times in quick succession. For example, if the referee blows the whistle three times, people try to get into a group of three, just like in Clumps. Anyone who is in a group of three cannot be tagged. IT should have approximately thirty seconds to tag as many as possible. When the whistle is blown again, everyone starts milling around again, safe for the moment. The referee then blows the whistle again a certain number of times, and again everyone must get into the appropriate size group and lock arms to be safe. The game continues with the referee constantly changing the numbers whistled. There will almost always be extra people running around madly without a group and its safety. If you have a PA system, or if the referee can shout loud enough, the game could be played by simply shouting the appropriate number rather than using the whistle. Those people who are tagged must leave the game, and the winner or winners are those people left when either the time is up or there are no more people to tag. For larger groups, you might have more than one IT. A good idea is for IT to have a crazy hat, shirt, or something that would help everyone identify him.

CRAZY BASKETBALL

Divide your entire group into two teams with any number of players. The game is played on a regular basketball court, without regular basketball rules. In this game, anything goes. The object is to score the most baskets any way you can. You can run, pass, dribble, or throw the basketball with no restrictions. For example, kids can ride piggyback for height. This game plays best with fifty to two hundred participants.

DOMINO

This is a great game that is not only fun to play, but fun to watch as well. It's also easy to play and requires no props. Teams line up in single-file lines parallel to each other. There should be the same number of people in each line, and everyone should face toward the front of the line. At a signal (whistle, etc.), the first person in each line squats, then each person in turn squats, all the way down to the end of the team's line. (You cannot squat down until the person immediately in front of you squats first.) The last person in line squats and then quickly stands up again, and in reverse, each person stands up in succession, instead of squatting. (Again, you cannot stand up until the person behind you first stands up.) The first team with the person standing at the front of the line is the winner.

This game looks much like playing standing dominoes where each domino falls in succession, except here the dominoes first go down, then back up again. It works best with at least twenty or so in each line (the more the better). Have the group try it several times for speed.

FOUR TEAM DODGEBALL

This is a fast-moving game that is best played in a gym or similar room. Divide the group into four teams of equal size. If you have a basketball court marked on the floor, this can be used as the playing area;

otherwise, you will need to mark off your own boundaries with tape or by some other method. The floor is divided into quadrants similar to the diagram below:

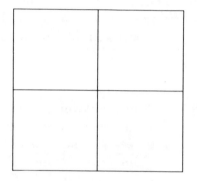

Each team is assigned one of the four areas, and team members cannot leave their assigned area during the game. A volleyball, beach ball, or playground ball should be used (nothing as hard as a basketball). The rules are basically the same as regular dodgeball, except that a player may throw the ball at anyone in any of the other three quadrants. If a player is hit below the belt with the ball, he is out of the game. If the ball misses and goes out-of-bounds, the referee tosses the ball into the team where it went out-of-bounds. If a player catches the ball before it hits the floor, without dropping it, the player who threw it is out. The winning team is the team that still has at least one player after the other teams have been eliminated or the team with the most players left at the end of a specified time limit.

GARBAGE BAG BALL

For this game, take a large plastic garbage bag and fill it full of balloons (blown-up) and tie it. You now have a Garbage Bag Ball. Here's an exciting game that makes good use of it.

Have all but ten of your group form a large circle on their knees. The remaining ten kids then form a pinwheel formation in the center of the circle, lying on their backs, heads toward the center. Everyone should have his shoes off for best results.

The garbage bag ball is then tossed into the circle. The object is for the kids on their backs to kick or hit the ball out of the circle, over the heads of the kids in the outer circle. The outer circle tries to keep it in play. If the ball is kicked over a player's head in the outer circle, then he must take the person's place in the inner circle. Play for as long as you wish.

Another game you can play with a "garbage bag ball" is Garbage Bag Volleyball, using regular volleyball rules.

GRAPE TOSS

Divide into teams of about ten. Each team gets into a circle and appoints one member to be the grape tosser. He gets a bag of grapes (or small marshmallows if you prefer) and stands in the center of the circle. When the signal is given, he tosses a grape to each team member in the circle, one at a time, and the team member must catch the grape in his mouth. The tosser cannot toss to the next player until a successful catch is made. The first team to toss all the way around the circle is the winner.

HUMAN SCAVENGER HUNT

Divide into teams and have each team choose a leader. All team members must stay within a designated area. A judge stands in a position that is equidistant from all teams. For example, if there are four teams, then the teams can position themselves in the four corners of the room and the judge can stand in the middle.

The judge calls a characteristic similar to the ones below, and the leader on each team tries to locate someone on the team that fits the characteristic. As soon as someone is found, the leader grabs that person by the hand, and they both run like crazy to the judge. The first team leader to slap the hand of the judge (pulling along the proper person) wins points for the team.

Here are some sample characteristics: Someone who. . . .
1. Has blue eyes and brown hair.
2. Received all A's on their last report card.
3. Ate at McDonald's today.
4. Jogs daily.
5. Is going steady.
6. Likes broccoli.
7. Sent a friend a card today.
8. Memorized a Bible verse this week.

9. Visited a foreign country this year.
10. Is wearing Nike sneakers.
11. Is chewing gum.
12. Came in a blue car.
13. Was stopped by a cop for a traffic violation this month.
14. Has a zit on his nose.
15. Received a love letter today.

INDOOR MURDERBALL

For this game, you need a room that is nearly indestructible, with plenty of room to run. Two teams of equal size line up on opposite walls, about three feet from the wall. Team members then number off.

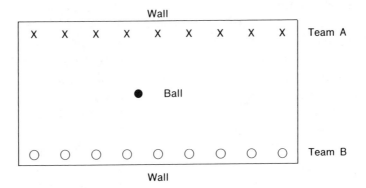

A ball is placed in the middle of the room. (Any large ball will work.) The leader calls a number, and the two players with that number (one from each team) run to the middle and try to hit the opposing team's wall with the ball. The team standing in front of the wall tries to stop the ball.

Players attempt to get the ball to its goal any way they can—carrying it across, throwing, kicking, rolling, whatever. Anything is legal.

INDOOR SCAVENGER HUNT

Divide the group into teams. Each team gets into one corner of the room with you in the middle. Each team appoints a runner who runs items from the team to you. You call various items that might be in the group, and each team tries to locate that item among team members, then gives it to the runner who then runs it to you. The first team to produce the named item wins one hundred points, and after twenty or so items, the team with the most points wins. Make sure that the runners all are running approximately the same distance. Here are some sample items you can call:

A white comb
A red sock
A 1969 penny
A student body card
An eyelash curler
A white T-shirt
A shoestring (without the shoe)
Four belts all tied together
Dark glasses
Picture of a rock star
A twenty-dollar bill
Some beef jerky
Denture adhesive
A hat

A turquoise ring or bracelet
The smelliest sock you can find (judge to decide winner)
A stick of gum
A theater ticket
A picture of your mother
A blue sweater
Toenail clippers
A book of matches
A cowboy boot
Forty-six cents exactly
A handkerchief
A Timex watch
A book with no pictures

KING OF THE CIRCLE

This game is always a winner, especially with boys. It is a very physical game. Simply draw a circle on the floor (or a square for KING OF THE SQUARE) and have everyone get inside. Then on "go," the object is to throw everyone else out of the circle while trying to stay in yourself.

The last person to stay in the circle is the winner. You will need referees to insure safety and to watch for players who allow any part of their bodies to touch outside the circle (they are out).

KING OF THE GOATS

Choose a "goat" from the group (or one from each team) and have it removed while the groups are given instruction. The crowd (one group) is instructed to stand on the sidelines and shout instructions to the goat, while the circle group (the other group) is told to form a circle holding hands. The goat is to be put in the center of the circle blindfolded. At the signal, the goat is to start chasing the circle and the circle is to move as a whole to avoid being caught. When the goat is ready to start, the circle group is instructed in its presence to move silently and to make no sound. The goat is to listen to the sideline crowd for instructions where to go to catch the circle. As soon as the start signal is given, the crowd starts shouting instructions to the goat, such as, "Go to the right, the right, now go back, go back, straight ahead." The minute the game starts, the circle team, instructed before the goat arrived, immediately disbands and joins the crowd, leaving the goat in an empty field. Let the goat run for a short time or until the goat guesses what is going on. Be sure you choose someone for this who is a "good sport."

KUBIC KIDS

This game is just the opposite of King of the Circle. Draw a square on the floor (as large or as small as you choose) and see how many kids each team can get inside the square. Anything is legal, as long as no part of the body is touching the floor outside the square. Set a time limit and have team competition.

LINE PULL

Divide the group into two equal teams. The teams then face each other on two sides of a line drawn on the floor. The object of the game is to pull the other team onto your side of the line. You cannot move behind your side of the line farther than three feet, and you must try to reach out and grab somebody on the other side of the line without stepping over the line. Once you are over the line, you are automatically a member of that team, then you must try to help pull the team you were once on over the line. At the end of the time period, the team with the largest number of kids wins.

MAD HATTER

Here's a free-for-all, which is really wild. Everybody should have a cap or hat. If you want the game to last longer, use ski caps. Then, give everybody a club (a sock stuffed full of cloth or something soft). When the signal is given, everybody tries to knock off everybody else's cap while keeping on his own. No hands may be used to protect yourself or your cap, and you may not knock off anyone's cap with anything except the sock club. When your cap is gone, you are out of the game. See who can last the longest.

MATH SCRAMBLE

Divide into teams. Each person wears a piece of paper with a number on it. (Numbers should begin at zero and end at the number of kids on the team.) The leader stands equidistant from each team and shouts a math problem, such as, "2 times 8 minus 4 divided by 3." The team must send the person wearing the correct answer (for example, the person wearing the number "4") to the leader. No team talking is allowed. The correct person must simply get up and run. The first correct answer to get to the leader wins one hundred points. The first team to reach one thousand points (or whatever) wins.

MUSICAL BACKS

This is a lot like musical chairs and similar elimination-type games. Kids simply mill about the room and when the music stops (or when the whistle blows, etc.), everyone quickly finds another person and stands back-to-back. When there are an odd number of people on the floor, someone will not have a partner and be eliminated. When there is an even number of people playing, a chair is placed on the floor, and anyone may sit in it and be safe. Naturally, every other time the chair will need to be removed. Make a rule that everyone must keep moving and players may not pair off with the same person twice in a row. The last person wins. It's a lot of fun.

MUSICAL GUYS

This game is played exactly like musical chairs, except guys are used in place of chairs. The guys form a circle, facing the center on their hands and knees. The girls (there should always be one more girl than the number of boys) stand behind the guys and at the start of the music (a whistle will work), the girls begin walking clockwise around the guys. When the music stops (or the whistle blows again), the girls grab any guy and jump on his back, horsey-style. The girl without a guy is out. The girls should be encouraged to "fight" for their guy. Play again with one less girl and one less guy in the circle. The last girl is the winner.

MUSICAL HATS

Pick six guys to stand in a circle, each facing the back of the guy in front. In other words, they would all be looking clockwise or all counterclockwise. Five of the guys put on hats (or you can use paper paint buckets), and when the music starts (or at a signal), each guy grabs the hat on the person's head in front of him and puts it on his own head. The hats are moving around the circle from head to head until the music stops (or the signal is given). Whoever is left without a hat is out of the game. Remove one hat and continue until there are only two guys left. They stand back-to-back, grabbing the hat off of each other's head, and when the music stops, the one wearing the hat is the winner.

MUSICAL SQUIRT GUN

This exciting game can be played with a group ranging from six to thirty, indoors or outdoors. Have the group sit in a circle either on chairs or on the floor. A loaded squirt gun is passed around the circle until the music stops or until the leader says, "Stop." The person who is holding the squirt gun at that time must leave the game. But before he leaves, he may squirt the person on his left twice or on his right twice or once each. After his chair is removed, the circle moves in, and the game continues. The last person left is declared the winner.

The gun must be passed with two hands and received with two hands (otherwise it will be frequently dropped and will break). It is best to have a second loaded squirt gun on hand to be substituted for the empty one. An assistant can refill the original gun, while the second one is being used. Be sure to emphasize that only two squirts are allowed, or you will be continually refilling the squirt guns.

PINCH ME

Here's a wild game (similar to Barnyard) that is great for dividing a large group into smaller groups. Everyone is to remain silent (no talking, but laughing, screaming, etc. is permitted). Each person receives a slip of paper that he is to keep secret from everyone else. The papers all read something like this:

Pinch Me	Step on My Toes
Slap Me	Rub My Tummy
Tickle Me	Scratch My Back
Pull My Ear	

When everyone has a card, the leader yells, "Go," and the players must find the others in their group. For instance, a Pinch Me must go around pinching everyone until he finds someone else who is a Pinch Me. They stick together pinching others until they find the rest of their team. There should be an equal number in each group. After a period of time, the leader stops the game, and the team that has done the best job of getting together wins.

PULL OFF

This is a wild game, which is easy to play and lots of fun. All the guys are to get inside a circle and huddle together in any position and lock arms. The girls attempt to pull the boys out of the circle any way they can. The guys try to stay in. The last guy to remain in the circle is the winner. Guys cannot fight the girls—only hang on and try to stay in.

PULL UP

For this game, everyone is seated in a circle, in chairs or on the floor, except for five girls and five boys who are in the middle (this number may vary depending on the total size of your group).

When the game starts, the ten kids in the middle run to someone of the opposite sex who is seated in the circle, grabs his hand, pulls the player up, and takes his place in the circle. The person who is pulled up cannot resist but must get up and run directly across the center of the circle to the other side and again pull up someone of the opposite sex and take his place in the circle.

The game continues until the leader blows a whistle, then everyone who is up must freeze instantly. The leader counts the number of boys who are up and how many girls are up. If there are more boys than girls, the girls get a point. If there are more girls than boys, the boys get a point. In other words, every time the whistle blows, the team (boys or girls) with the least number standing wins points.

PYRAMID CLUMPS

This game is like Clumps (page 77) but with one added twist. When the leader calls a number, players must not only get into a group of that size, but they must also build a pyramid with exactly that number in the pyramid. After a period of time, any pyramid that doesn't have the right number or whose players are not in it is eliminated. The game continues until there are only a few players left.

PYRAMID PLAY-OFFS

Divide into groups of six. A team receives points when they are first to complete the instructions given. They must form a complete pyramid and then do the instructions. Afterwards they must dismantle and begin when you say, "Go!" Scale your points according to the number in the pyramid involved in the action if you make up more instructions. Use directions such as these:

1. Form a pyramid and "ALL say the Pledge of Allegiance in unison."
2. The BOTTOM PERSON in the middle must take off his shoes.
3. The TWO PEOPLE ON THE SECOND LEVEL must turn completely around.
4. The PERSON ON THE TOP must comb through both sides of THE PERSON ON THE BOTTOM LEFT'S hair.
5. The PERSON ON THE SECOND LEVEL ON THE LEFT must turn around.
6. The MIDDLE PERSON ON THE BOTTOM must turn around.
7. The WHOLE TEAM turns around in a circle (only the bottom 3 have to move).

RAINBOW SOCCER

Here's an active game played with two teams and sixty balloons (thirty each of two colors). The balloons are mixed together and placed in the center circle of a regulation basketball court. The two teams line up on the end lines facing each other. One person from each team is the goalie and stands at the opposite end of the floor from his team, in front of a large container.

At the whistle, each team tries to kick (using soccer rules) their balloons to their goalie, who then puts them into the container behind him. To play defense, a team stomps and pops as many of the other team's balloons as possible. Play continues until all the balloons are scored or popped. The team with the most goals wins.

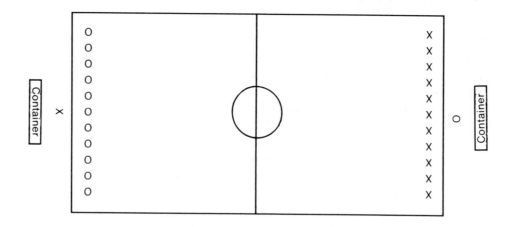

ROUND-UP

All the kids are divided into two teams with the same number of boys and girls on each team. The girls of each team are the cowboys; the boys the cows. The cows must stay on their hands and knees throughout the game. The object of the game is for the girls of each team to get the cows of the opposing team into an area designated as the corral. The girls can drag, carry, etc. a cow to the corral. Of course, the cows can resist but must stay on hands and knees. After a certain time interval, the team with the most cows in their corral wins the game.

SHOCK

This game is a lot like "Domino" (page 79). Two teams line up single file and hold hands. There has to be exactly the same number on each team. On one end of the team, there is a spoon on the floor (or on a table) and at the other end, there is a person from each team with a coin.

The two people with the coins begin flipping them (like a coin toss) and showing the coin to the first person in line on their team. If the coin is tails, nothing happens. If the coin is heads, the first person quickly squeezes the hand of the second person, who squeezes the hand of the third person, and so on down the line. As soon as the last person in line has his hand squeezed, he tries to grab the spoon. After grabbing the spoon, the spoon is replaced and that person then runs to the front of the line and becomes the coin flipper. Everybody else moves down one person. Play continues until every player has been the coin flipper and the spoon grabber. The first team to get its original coin flipper or spoon grabber back into their original positions is the winner.

No one may squeeze the next person's hand until his own hand has been squeezed first. This is like an electric shock that works its way down the line. A referee should be stationed at both ends of the team lines to make sure everything is done legally. A false shock results in a new coin flip. You might want to have everyone practice his squeeze before starting, so everyone knows to squeeze good and hard. Otherwise, someone might confuse a little twitch for a legal squeeze.

SING SONG SORTING

This game is similar to "Barnyard" (page 69) and is great as a way to divide a crowd into teams or small groups. Prepare ahead of time on small slips of paper an equal number of four (or however many groups you want) different song titles. As each person enters the room, they receive (at random) one of these song titles. In other words, if you had one hundred kids and you wanted four teams, there would be twenty-five each of the four different songs. At a signal, the lights are turned out (if you do this at night), and each kid starts singing as loudly as possible—no talking or yelling, only singing. Each person tries to locate others singing the same song, and the first team to get together is the winner. Song titles should be well-known.

SNOWFIGHT

This one creates quite a mess, but it's worth it. Divide into two teams and put a divider down the center of the room (like a couple of rows of chairs, back-to-back). The two teams are on the opposite sides of the divider. Give each team a large stack of old newspapers, then give them five or ten minutes to prepare their "snow" by wadding the paper into balls—the more, the better.

When the signal to begin is given, players start tossing their snow at the opposing team, which really does look like a snowstorm. When the whistle blows, everyone must stop throwing. Judges determine the winner by deciding which team has the least amount of snow on its side of the divider.

With larger groups, watch out for players who lose their eyeglasses or other personal belongings in the snow, which gets pretty deep. After the game is over, provide plastic garbage bags and have a race to see which side can stuff all their snow into the bags first.

SPACEBALL COUNTDOWN

Here is a fast, exciting, and rough game that requires teamwork, and kids love it. Form two equal teams with one team forming an evenly spaced rectangle or circle and the other team inside the circle as dispersed as possible. When the whistle sounds, the team outside tries to hit with the ball (two playground balls, not soccer balls) every member inside as quickly as possible. Head hits and bounce hits are illegal.

When everyone has been hit, the clock stops, the time is recorded, and the teams change places. The team with the shortest time in the outside circle wins. You can score the best two out of three rounds or combine total times. Be sure to have players remove glasses, aim shoulder level and below, and do not use hard, soccer-type balls.

SPELLER

This is another game that is very similar to "Clumps" (page 77). Give everyone a large letter of the alphabet to wear. If you prefer, mark the letter on the person's forehead using a marker that will wash off. Avoid the use of uncommon letters like Q, X, Z, and the like.

Players should mingle around, and when the whistle is blown, the leader shouts a number, like "three." Players then must find two other players and form a word using their letters. Any players who are unable to become part of a three letter word within a reasonable amount of time are eliminated from the game. For obvious reasons, you need to keep the numbers small enough that words can be formed.

SQUATTERS SMASH

This is a simple elimination game that can get physical. It can be played coed or as a boys-only/girls-only game. Players squat down on their heels and fold their arms. They must stay in that position during the entire game. The object is to walk around and knock the other players off-balance. A player is out of the game if he falls over. Anything is legal, so long as players stay in the squatting, arms-crossed position.

SQUIRREL

For this game, everyone gets into a small group of four. Three of the four join hands and become a hollow tree. The fourth person is a squirrel who gets inside the hollow tree (inside the circle formed by his teammates).

Two extra players are needed—another squirrel and a hound. When the game begins, the hound chases the extra squirrel in and out between the trees. For safety, the squirrel may crawl into any tree, but the squirrel already in that tree must leave and flee from the hound. If the hound tags the free squirrel, the squirrel becomes the hound, the hound becomes the squirrel, and the game continues.

STACK 'EM UP

Have everyone sit in chairs in a circle. Prepare a list of qualifying characteristics such as these:

1. If you forgot to use a deodorant today, . . .
2. If you got a traffic ticket this year, . . .
3. If you have a hole in your sock, . . .
4. If you are afraid of the dark, . . .

Then read them one at a time and add "move three chairs to the right," "move one chair to the left," etc. In other words, you might say, "If you forgot to use a deodorant today, *move three chairs to the right,*" and all those who "qualify" move as instructed and sit in that chair, regardless of whether or not it's occupied by one or more persons. As the game progresses, kids begin stacking up on certain chairs.

STREETS AND ALLEYS

This is another tag game, which a lot of fun. One person is IT and chases another player through a maze of people. The other players form the maze in this manner:

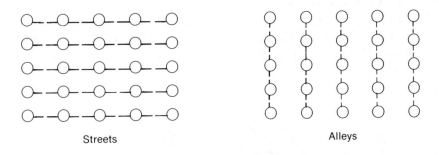

Streets   Alleys

Everyone in the maze is facing in one direction, hands joined, forming alleys. When the leader shouts, "Streets!", they all do a right face and grasp hands again in the other direction. The person who is IT tries to catch the runner, but cannot cross the joined hands. When the leader calls, "Alleys!", the players in the maze assume their original position. The game continues with several players getting a chance to be IT and to be the chasee.

TECHNICOLOR STOMP

Here's a good indoor game, which is really wild. You will need lots of colored balloons. Divide into teams and assign each team a color (red, blue, orange, yellow, etc.). Then give each team an equal number of balloons of their color. For example, the red team would be given a certain number (like twenty) red balloons. They begin by blowing up all the balloons and tying them. When the actual game begins, the balloons from all the teams are released onto the floor, and the object is to stomp on and pop all the balloons of the *other* teams while attempting to protect your own team's balloons. After the time is up (two or three minutes should do it), the popping of balloons stops, and each team gathers up its remaining balloons. The team with the most balloons left is the winner.

TINY TIM RACE

Divide the group into teams. At a signal, each team must line up according to height, with the shortest person on one end and the tallest on the other. The last team to do so or any team that is out of the proper order is the loser.

TOE FENCING

Here's a wild game, and if it's set to music, it looks like a new kind of dance. All the players pair off, lock hands, and try to tap the top of one of their partner's feet with their own feet. In other words, one player tries to stomp on the other player's foot while their hands are clasped (tapping sounds a bit more humane). Of course, since players are also trying to avoid having their feet stepped on, they are all hopping around the floor in a frantic dance.

When a player has had his foot tapped three times, he is out of the game, and the winning partner challenges another winner. The game continues until only one person is left (or until the music runs out).

WEATHER BALLOON VOLLEYBALL

Two teams of any number can play this funny volleyball game that uses a giant weather balloon for a ball. Six to eight feet in diameter, the balloon is inflated with a vacuum cleaner. The entire team gets under the ball and pushes it over the net. The opposing team returns it. Giant weather balloons are available from army surplus stores and other specialty shops. Other types of giant balloons can also be used. It's best to play this game indoors because a light wind can carry your balloon a long way.

5.

ACTIVE
INDOOR GAMES
FOR
SMALL GROUPS

All of the games in this chapter are great for playing indoors with groups of thirty or less. They are not limited to thirty but they are best played with small numbers. Some require a big indoor space, like a gymnasium or fellowship hall, while others can be played in much smaller space.

Keep in mind that there are many other good, active indoor games for small groups in chapters 7 and 3. Most outdoor games can be easily adapted for indoor use. There are lots of less active games for small groups in chapter 8. And of course, many other games throughout this book can be easily adapted for use with small groups in an indoor setting.

BACK TO BACK
Divide your group into pairs and have them sit on the floor back-to-back and link arms. Then tell them to stand up. With a little timing and cooperation, it shouldn't be too hard. Then combine two pairs into a foursome. Have the foursome sit on the floor back-to-back with arms linked. Tell them to stand up. It is a little harder with four. Keep adding more people to the group until the giant blob can't stand up any more.

ALPHABET-PONG

For this game, the group arranges itself into a circle. Each person holds a book with both hands. One player takes a Ping-pong ball, hits it with the book across the circle, and calls, "A." The person on the other side then returns it to someone and calls, "B," and so forth. The circle works together to see how far down the alphabet they can call before they miss. There is no particular order for hitting the ball. Anyone can hit it when it comes to them, but no one may hit the ball twice in a row. For teams, have the first team try it and then the other to see which one can get the farthest down the alphabet without the ball hitting the floor. It's a real challenge!

BALANCING BRONCOS

Divide your group into two or more teams. The guys are the horses, and the girls are the riders. The object of the game is for a girl to sit cross-legged (Indian-style) on the boy's back. He must go around an obstacle and back without her falling off. If she falls off, they must start again at either the beginning or back at the halfway point. The girls can't hang on. They must try to balance. It is easier if they face backward. If after you divide into teams, you have more guys than girls, then the game is over when one team has sent all its guys around the obstacle. (You'll have to use some girls twice.) If the ratio is the other way, then all the girls have to ride. (You'll have to use some boys more than once.) This game moves quickly and is a lot more challenging than it sounds.

BALLOON BLOWER BASKETBALL

For this game, you'll need a basketball court, several basketballs, and several large balloons. Have one team line up behind the free throw line at one end of the basketball court and one team at the other end. Each team designates someone as their balloon blower. At the signal, the first person in line shoots a basketball from the free throw line or dribbles as close as he wants to the net and shoots. The second person in line must stay behind the free throw line until the ball is thrown back by the person who just shot. After shooting, players get back in line. Each time someone makes a basket, the balloon blower makes one giant blow into the balloon. The team that pops their balloon first wins. If you want the game to go longer, you can give each team two or three balloons.

BALLOON BURST

Divide your group into two teams and pick a captain for each. Arrange them as diagrammed below. Each team tries to hit the balloon in the direction of their captain, who will then burst the balloon with a pin. One point is scored for each balloon burst. Players must stay seated and use only one hand.

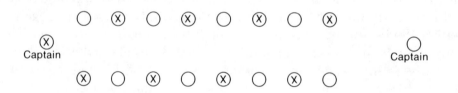

BASKETBALL SQUAT

Divide your group into teams (approximately six to ten per team). Have the teams choose a captain for each group and line up in a straight line facing the captains (approximately five to ten feet away from the captains). The captain throws the ball to the first person in the line who returns the throw and then squats down. The captain then throws the ball to the second person who does the same and on down the line to the last person. The captain then throws the ball a second time to the last person who throws it back and stands back up. Play continues until everyone has received another pass, working its way up to the first person in line. Any time the ball is dropped, the team must start all over again. The first team to get everybody standing up again is the winner.

BLACKOUT

Here's a new twist to musical chairs, which is a real riot. First arrange the chairs in a circle facing outward. Players form a circle around the outside of the chairs. Explain that players must keep their hands behind their backs. The boys must walk around the chairs clockwise, while the girls are to move counterclockwise when the music starts or when the whistle blows. When the music stops, participants must sit down on the closest empty chair available. There's one catch—the game is played in the dark. When the music starts, turn the lights out. When the music stops, turn the lights on. Be prepared for a lot of scrambling, and running for chairs. The person left standing is out. Be sure to take one chair out after each round and move the remaining chairs closer together as the group gets smaller. Kids have a lot of fun playing this, and usually the girls are more aggressive than the boys.

BLIND VOLLEYBALL

Divide the kids into two equal teams. The two teams then get on each side of a volleyball court and sit down either on chairs or on the floor in rows, arranged like regular volleyball. The net should be a solid divider that obstructs the view of the other team, such as blankets hung over a regular volleyball net or rope. The divider should also be low enough that players cannot see under it. Then play volleyball. Use a big, light plastic ball instead of a volleyball. Regular volleyball rules and boundaries apply. A player cannot stand up to hit the ball. The added dimension of the solid net adds a real surprise element to the game when the ball comes flying over the net.

BLINDMAN BACON

This variation of "Steal the Bacon" (page 60) plays best in a circle. Two teams of equal size number off, so there is a player on each team for each number. When a number is called, the corresponding player for each team puts on a blindfold. After hearing the whistle, both players go to the middle of the circle and, with the guidance of screams from teammates, they both try to locate a squirt gun lying in the middle of the circle. Once the squirt gun is found, each player then tries to squirt the other player before that player can escape out of the circle, behind his teammates. If the player with the squirt gun successfully shoots the other player, a point is awarded to his team. If the other player escapes, his team is awarded the point.

The game is made more exciting if, after the blindfolds go on, the leader moves the squirt gun, making it more difficult to locate.

BEAN BLITZ

This is a good way to get kids involved with each other at the beginning of a meeting or social event. Each kid is given an envelope containing twenty beans. The kids wander around the room holding in their closed hands a few beans from the envelope. They approach other kids, one at a time, and ask, "Odd or Even?" referring to the beans in their hand. If the person they ask guesses correctly, he gets the beans. If he guesses wrong, he must give up the same number of beans. (He is required to guess *only whether the number is odd or even*, not what the actual number of beans is.) A time limit is set, and whoever has the most beans at the end wins a prize. When your beans are all gone, you are out.

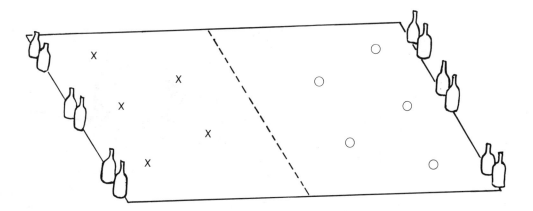

BOTTLEBALL

This game can be played indoors or outdoors. The ideal number for this game is five for each side, but it can be adapted for more, depending on the size of your group. Make distinguishable boundaries, approximately sixty feet by thirty feet. The three end players must guard two bottles each. (The large plastic pop bottles work ideally.) These bottles should be placed about eighteen inches apart. The throwers try to shoot a medium size Nerf basketball (or another soft-type ball) through the opposite side, their opponents blocking the ball as best they can. Players foul when they step beyond the midway line. The scoring goes like this: five points for each bottle knocked down; ten points for each shot that goes between the bottles; one point for each shot rolling over the back boundary line. Divide your group into four, six, or eight different teams and have a tournament.

CHAIRBALL

This game is an exciting version of basketball that can be played on any open field or large room. Instead of using a regular basketball, use a ball

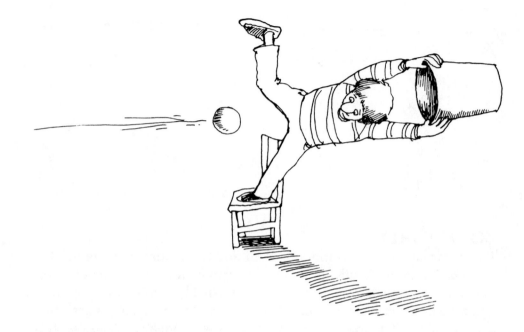

that is a bit lighter, like a playground ball or a Nerf ball. You may have any number of people on the two teams. At each end of the playing area, have someone standing on a chair holding a wastebasket or a similar container. A jump ball starts the game, just like regular basketball. The players then try to move the ball down the field to shoot a basket. The person on the chair who is holding the basket may try to help by moving the basket, if necessary, to catch the ball when it is shot. All shots must be made beyond a ten-foot foul line. The ball may only be moved downfield by throwing it to a teammate or by kicking it. You may not run or walk with the ball. You may score baskets just like regular basketball or with any point system that you choose.

CHINESE PING-PONG

Here's a good way to add some excitement to an ordinary game of Ping-Pong. Have your entire group (up to a dozen or so kids) stand around a regular Ping-Pong table. One player should be on each end of the table; the others are at the sides. The first person serves the ball, just like regular Ping-Pong, but after he serves it, he puts the paddle down on the table (with the handle sticking over the edge) and gets in the line to his left. The next person in line (to the server's right) picks up the paddle and waits for the ball to be returned. The line keeps rotating around the table in a clockwise fashion, with each person hitting the ball once from whichever end of the table he happens to be. If he drops the paddle, misses the ball, or hits it off the table, he is eliminated from the game. When it gets down to the last two people, they must hit the ball, put the paddle down, turn completely around, pick up the paddle, and hit the ball. The last player to make a mistake is the winner.

CINDERELLA

Arrange chairs in a circle. All the Cinderellas (girls) in the group select a chair. The Prince Charmings (guys) each pick a Cinderella and kneel down in front of her. He removes her shoes and holds them in his hand. The leader calls for the shoes, and they are thrown to the middle of the circle. Then the Cinderellas blindfold their Prince Charmings. After each prince is blindfolded, the leader rearranges and mixes the shoes in the middle.

At a signal, all the Prince Charmings crawl to the circle and attempt to find their Cinderellas' shoes. The Cinderellas can help only verbally, shouting instructions to their men. After finding the shoes, the princes crawl back to their girls (again guided by verbal instructions). They place the shoes (right one on right foot, etc.) on the girls and then remove their blindfolds. The game continues until the last contestant succeeds.

CLOTHESPIN CHALLENGE

This is a simple game for teams of two. They are seated in chairs facing each other with their knees touching. Each is shown a large pile of clothespins at the right of his chair. Each is blindfolded and given two minutes to pin as many clothespins as possible on the pant legs of the other contestant.

CONTEST OF THE WINDS

Draw a large square on the floor similar to the diagram below. The square is divided into four equal parts, designated as the North, East, South and West. Divide the group into four teams of the same names. Scatter dried leaves (or cotton balls) evenly in each quarter of the square. At a given signal, the "winds begin to blow," and each team tries to *blow* (no hands allowed) the leaves out of their square into another. Set a time limit, and the team with the least leaves in their square wins.

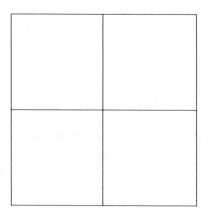

DICE GRAB

To play this game, you will need to buy some oversized dice at a game or stationery store or, if you want to make your own, cut two small blocks of wood into 1 1/4'" cubes. Sand and paint them if you wish, then mark them with dots similar to a pair of dice.

Mark a two-foot diameter circle with chalk on the floor, or on a rug, or on the top of a card table. One person starts the game by rolling the dice toward the center and simultaneously calling any single number between two and twelve. If the dots total the number called, all may grab for them. Each die is worth one point on the grab, and the scramble may continue out of the circle or off the table.

The game becomes more exciting as the time between throws is lessened. The roller continues until the number he calls is thrown, then he passes the dice to an adjacent player. A game is usually won when someone earns eleven points.

DOWN THE DRAIN

For this game, you'll need to get quite a few of those plastic tubes that protect the clubs found in most golf club bags. You can probably borrow these from someone because the game won't damage them.

Divide the group into two equal teams. Each team gets half the tubes or one for each player. The teams line up, and the players hold the tubes end-to-end, using their hands to secure the joints.

At the beginning of each line, the team leaders or sponsors simultaneously place a marble in the end of the first tube. The object is for the team to move the marble down all the tubes and out the other end. The team that is first to do this is the winner. If the marble slips through one of the joints and falls onto the floor, the team is disqualified. Once the kids get the hang of it, they should be able to do it rather smoothly. There is some strategy involved, however, and the kids will enjoy the challenge.

To make the game a little longer, go for the best two out of three, or give each team ten marbles to send "down the drain." Only one marble is allowed in the drain at a time. Somebody should be assigned to catch the marbles when they come out.

DUCKIE WUCKIE

Everyone sits in a circle with one person standing in the middle. The person in the middle is blindfolded and has a rolled-up newspaper. He is spun around as everyone else changes seats. (Everyone needs to be silent.) The person blindfolded then finds a person's lap *only* by means of the newspaper, unfolds it, places it on the lap, and sits on the newspaper and says, "Duckie wuckie." In a disguised voice, the person being sat upon responds, "Quack-quack." This may be repeated twice more. After each "Quack-quack," the blindfolded person may guess the identity of the voice. If correct, the voice gets the blindfold; if incorrect, the blindfold must find another lap and try again.

DUNCE BOMBERS

Here's an indoor game that kids (especially junior highs) will scream for again and again. Two teams are chosen at random and seated on opposite sides of the room. Each team has a dunce, who sits with a styrofoam cup balanced on his head, somewhere near the back of the group. All players must stay seated in one spot throughout the game. The object of the game is to knock the cup off the head of the other team's dunce with wadded newspaper. The dunce cannot use his hands in any way, but other team members can bat down flying paper bombs as long as their seats don't leave the ground. A point is scored each time a team knocks off the other team's dunce cap. Kids can be very creative using a variety of large and small bombs, paper airplanes, machine gun blasts, cooperative barrages, protective seating, paper clubs to knock down bombs, etc. The game usually takes a stack of newspaper about four feet high.

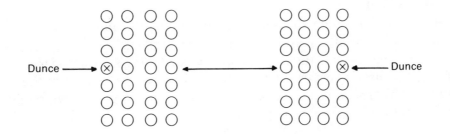

ELECTRIC FENCE

For this game, you need two poles and a piece of rope or string. The rope is tied between the two poles, about two feet off the floor to begin.

Divide into teams. The object of the game is for the entire team to get over the electric fence (the rope) without getting electrocuted (touching the rope). Each team takes a turn, with team members going one-at-a-time.

After each successful try, the rope is raised a little higher, as in regular high jump competition. Eventually, teams will be eliminated as they find the rope too high to get over.

What makes this game interesting is that even though one player goes over the rope at a time, the other team members can help any way they want. Once a person is over the fence, however, he must stay over the fence and not come back around to help anyone. So the last person each time must somehow get over the fence without help on one side. This game requires lots of teamwork and cooperation.

Teams can be eliminated entirely if one person touches the fence; individual members can be eliminated only as the rope gets higher and

113

higher. Make sure your teams are evenly divided according to height, age, and sex.

ESKINOSE

Teams line up boy-girl-boy-girl. One person on the end of each line gets a lipstick smear on the end of his nose. The idea is to see how far down the line you can pass the lipstick smear by rubbing noses. The team that can get it the farthest or the team that can get it the farthest in the time limit (thirty seconds, for example) is the winner. A good prize might be Eskimo Pies.

FEETBALL

This is a good indoor game, which is very active and requires teamwork. Divide the group into teams and seat them in two lines of chairs, facing each other. The object is for the teams to move a volleyball or similar ball toward and through their goal (at the end of the line) by using their feet only. Players must keep their arms behind the chairs to keep from touching the ball, which is a penalty. To begin the game, drop the ball between the two teams in the middle. The game can be any length desired. To avoid injuries to feet, shoes can be removed. Also, make sure the two teams are just far enough apart that their feet barely touch when legs are extended on both sides.

FRUITBASKET UPSET

This game can be played with any number of people, usually indoors. The entire group sits in an approximate circle with one less chair than there are people. The extra person stands in the middle. Everyone is secretly assigned the name of a fruit. The person in the middle begins by calling several of the fruits. After naming several fruits, he yells,

"Go," and those people who were assigned the fruits called must change chairs. At the same time the person in the middle also tries to get one of the vacant chairs. The person who fails to get a chair is then the one in the middle. As an option, the person in the middle may call, "Fruitbasket upset." Then everyone must change chairs. Be sure to use sturdy chairs because people usually land in other people's laps.

GOOFY GOLF

Set up a miniature golf course all over your playing area. If you are using a church building, make your course travel down hallways, in and out of rooms, down staircases, and the like. For golf balls, use either real balls, balloons with a marble inside (they take unusual rolls), old stale marshmallows, Ping-pong balls, or whiffle golf balls. For clubs, use golf clubs, broom handles, rolled-up newspapers, etc.

Each hole should be marked with a flag, as in regular golf, and tees should also be designated. Set par for each hole, print up some scorecards, and have a Goofy Golf Tournament.

GORILLA-MAN-GUN

This game is a lot like the old paper-rock-scissors game kids play. Have everyone in your group pair off and stand in two lines, with each couple across from each other, back-to-back.

X	X	X	X	X	X	X	X	X
O	O	O	O	O	O	O	O	O

The leader, who merely directs the action, shouts, "One, two, three!" And on "three," everybody turns around and instantly assumes one of three positions:
1. GORILLA—hands up in air, teeth snarling, and shouts, "Grrroowwwlll."

2. MAN—hands on hips, says, "Hi, there."
3. GUN—both hands draw imaginary guns from hips, shoot, and he shouts, "Bang!"

When the leader says, "Three," each person turns around and takes one of the above positions as he is *turning around* to face his partner. No one can hesitate. Then each couple decides which of them won, determined by one of the following ways:

a. If one person is MAN and one is GUN, the MAN wins because a man has the power over the gun.
b. If one person is GUN and the other is GORILLA, the gun wins because the gorilla can be shot by the gun.
c. If one person is GORILLA and one is MAN, gorilla wins because the gorilla is stronger than the man.
d. If both persons are the SAME, they try again. (Both win.) If they tie a second time, both lose.

After the first try, all the losers are out. All the winners pair up again, and the game continues until the last couple plays and the winner is determined. It is best to demonstrate this game several times to the group before playing.

HA-HA-HA GAME

This is a crazy game that is good for a lot of laughs (literally). One person lies down on the floor (on his back), the next person lies down with his head on the first person's stomach, and the next person lies down with his head on the second person's stomach, and so on.

After everyone is down on the floor, the first person says, "Ha," the second says, "Ha Ha," and the third says, "Ha Ha Ha," and so on. It is to be played *seriously*, and if anyone goofs it and laughs, the group must start over. It's hilarious.

HAND OVER HAND

Divide your group into two or more teams of five or more participants. Each team forms a circle, and everyone holds his right hand in the middle of the circle. Have them stack their hands basketball-huddle-style. Then have them place their left hands in the circle in the same manner so that left hands are stacked on top of the right hand stack. At the signal, the person whose hand is on the bottom should take that hand and place it on top of the stack. The next person should do the same, and so on until the person who began the process is again on the bottom. The first team to complete this process is winner of round #1. For the next round, try three laps, then try five. After everyone is getting the hang of it, try going backward.

HOT TOWEL

Everyone sits in a circle, and one person in the center of the circle is IT. IT tosses a towel to someone sitting in the circle, and then the towel is passed around the circle in any direction. The object of the game is for IT to tag whoever is holding the towel. When he catches somebody with the towel, they exchange positions. The towel keeps moving, which makes this very difficult, unless someone is having trouble getting rid of it. If it is passed to you, you must take it. Part of the fun is when someone passes the towel by looping it around the next person's neck or arm, which makes it hard to undo in a hurry. If the towel is caught by IT in midair (while it is being tossed to someone), the player who threw it becomes the new IT.

HUMAN TIC-TAC-TOE

As suggested by its title, this game is played just like it is on paper, except that people are used. It is very active and great for smaller groups. To play, set up nine chairs in three rows of three. Team One stands on one side of the chairs, and Team Two on the other. Players on each team then number off.

The leader calls a number, like "four." As soon as the number is called, the two fours on each team scramble to sit down in any two chairs as quickly as they can. When they are seated, another number is called, and play continues until three teammates from either team have successfully scored a tic-tac-toe by sitting in a row of three either up, down, or diagonally. If no tic-tac-toe is made, then the players return to their team, and the game is played again.

A variation of this would be to play with ten people per game (five on a team). They all take a seat in one of the nine chairs, leaving one person without a seat. When the whistle is blown, everyone must get up and move to a different chair, while the extra person tries to sit down somewhere. After the mad scramble for seats, the game is scored like tic-tac-toe. Any row of three people from the same team gets points. Each round, there will always be one person left without a seat.

An even crazier way to play this game would be to play as described above, but use guys on their hands and knees as chairs and have girls from each team sit on the guys' backs. When the whistle is blown, each girl jumps on a guy and tries to hang on, even though another girl may try to pull her off or take the same guy. It's really wild. Whether you use chairs, guys, lines on the floor (like real tic-tac-toe) or whatever, it's a lot of fun to play.

HUNTERS AND HOUNDS

Kids pair off—one being the hunter, and the other being the hound. The hunters each get a shoebox (or similar box), and the hounds try to go out and find (for the hunters) peanuts which have been hidden beforehand around the room. When a hound finds a peanut, he cannot touch it but begins to howl, and his corresponding hunter comes and retrieves the peanut. When two or more hounds find the same peanut, each howls, and the hunter who gets there first gets the nut. All hunters wait in the "lodge" (a circle or specified area where they wait for their hounds to howl).

INDOOR SOCCER

Clear out an open space on the floor and have everyone get down on his hands and knees. There should be two teams. Goals should be marked on both ends of the room. A feather or a Ping-Pong ball is placed between the two teams, and the players try to blow the feather or the Ping-Pong ball across the other team's goal line. No hands are allowed. Limit this game to about five or six per team.

INDOOR VOLLEYBALL

You can play an exciting volleyball game inside, even with a low ceiling, by using a Nerf basketball (about eight inches in diameter). Hang up a regular net, drape sheets across a rope, or stack up tables between the two teams. For low ceilings, keep the net low and have everyone play while sitting on the floor or on his knees. Other volleyball rules apply.

INVERSION

This game requires a great deal of teamwork. It can be played as a competitive game (teams compete against each other) or as a cooperative game (everyone is on the same team).

Draw two parallel lines on the floor about eighteen inches apart. The team lines up inside those two lines and number off. At a signal, they must reverse their number order without stepping outside those two parallel lines. For example, if there are twenty people on the team, then player number 1 must change places with player number 20, and so on. Only the person in the middle stays in the same place.

18" ① ② ③ ④ ⑤ ⑥ ⑦ ⑧ ⑨ ⑩ ⑪ ⑫ ⑬ ⑭

Let the teams practice this once and come up with a strategy for doing it quickly and accurately. Then compete against the clock to set a "World Record" for the youth group or see which team can do it in the quickest time. It's a lot of fun to watch. Referees can penalize a team in seconds lost whenever a person steps outside one of the two lines.

LET IT BLOW
Divide your group into teams and give each person a deflated balloon. At a signal, the first person on each team blows up his balloon and lets it go. The balloon will sail through the air.

That person must then go to where it lands, stop, and blow it up again and let it go. The object is to get the balloon across a goal line some distance away. When he does, the player can run back and tag the next player on the team, then that person must do the same thing. This game is really wild since it is almost impossible to predict where the balloons will land each time. It is especially fun and interesting when

121

played outside because the slightest breeze blows the balloon in a different direction. The goal line should be about fifteen feet away.

LONGJOHN STUFF

This is a hilarious game that is always fun with any group. You will need to get two pairs of long underwear and about one hundred small (six inch round) balloons. You will also need a straight pin. Divide into two teams. Each team selects one person from their team to put on a pair of longjohns. It would be best for them to pick someone who is not too big. The longjohns should just go on over the kid's regular clothes. Each team should also select two or three balloon stuffers.

When the kids are ready, throw out an equal number of balloons to the two teams. The team members must blow them up (all the way), tie them, and pass them to the stuffers who try to stuff all of them into the longjohns. The object is to see which team can stuff the most balloons into their person's longjohns within the given time limit. Usually, about two minutes is long enough. After both contestants have been sufficiently stuffed, stop the two teams and have the two people in the longjohns stand still. (Now would be a good time for some pictures.)

To count the balloons, begin with the one who appears to have the fewest balloons and pop them with a pin (through the longjohns), while the team counts. (Be careful you don't stick the contestant with the pin.)

MAD ADS

This game is similar to the "Indoor Scavenger Hunt" (page 84). Divide into teams and give each team a magazine (the same issue of the same magazine for all teams). Ahead of time, the leader should make a list of about thirty or forty advertisements throughout the magazine (big ones and small ones).

The teams should be instructed to tear the pages out of the magazine and divide them up between the team members. They can spread them out on the floor if they want. The leader stands an equal distance from all the teams and calls the name of an advertisement. The first team to locate the ad, hand it to their runner, and get it to the leader wins the designated number of points. The team scoring the most points wins.

A couple of tips: If one team is slaughtering the others, increase the point value of ads later in the game, so the other teams can have a chance to catch up. Women's magazines are best for this game (*Ladies Home Journal*, etc.) because they seem to carry more ads than most magazines.

MAGAZINE SCAVENGER HUNT

Divide your group into teams of two or three persons each and give each group a combination of old magazines. Then give them a list of various items, such as photos, names, products, etc., that could be found in the magazines. As soon as a group finds one of the items, they cut it out and continue to collect as many as they can in the time limit. The list can be long or short depending on the time. Some of the items will be found in several magazines, while others in only one. You can make the list as difficult as you want. The winner, of course, is the team with the most items found.

MARSHMALLOW PITCH

For this game, have your kids pair off and give each pair a sack of miniature marshmallows. Each pair should also have a neutral counter. One person is the pitcher, the other the catcher. On ''go,'' the pitcher tosses a marshmallow into the catcher's mouth, and the catcher must eat the marshmallow. The pitcher and catcher should be about ten feet apart. The counter counts how many successful catches are made, and the couple with the most at the end of a time limit or the first to reach twenty successful catches is the winner.

MUSICAL COSTUMES

Here is a funny game that allows everyone to look a little silly. Before you start, have a laundry bag or pillow case filled with various articles of clothing—funny hats, baggy pants, gloves, belts, or anything that can be worn. (The leader can use his own discretion as to how embarrassing the items are.) Keep the bag tied shut, so the clothing will not spill out.

Have your group form a circle and start passing the bag around as music is played. (If you don't use music, use some other random signal like an egg timer or automatic toaster to stop the action.) When the music stops, the person holding the bag must reach in and take out an article without looking. Then he must put it on and wear it for the remainder of the game. Try to have enough, so each person gets three or four funny articles of clothing. This can lend itself to seasonal clothing, such as Santa's bag, Easter Parade, etc. It may also be a fun way to create an instant costume for a Halloween party. After the game, you can have a fashion show or take pictures to hang up on the group bulletin board.

PAPER SHOOT

Divide into teams of from four to eight kids each. Set a garbage can up in the middle of the room (about three feet high), and prepare ahead of time several paper batons and a lot of wadded-up paper balls. One team lies down around the trash can with their heads toward the can (on their backs). Each of these players has a paper baton. The opposing team stands around the trash can behind a line about ten feet or so away from the can. This line can be a large circle drawn around the can. The opposing team tries to throw the wadded-up paper balls into the can, and the defending team tries to knock the balls away with their batons while lying on their backs. The opposing team gets two minutes to try and shoot as much paper into the can as possible. After each team has had its chance to be in both positions, the team that got the most paper balls into the can is declared the winner. To make the game a bit more difficult for the throwers, have them sit in chairs while they toss the paper.

PINBALL SOCCER
Here's a new way to play soccer that is best played indoors. It's just like regular soccer, except that you give each person, including the goalie, a piece of paper to stand on and a particular place to put the paper. They must keep one foot on the paper at all times. Scooting the paper is not allowed. Be sure to scatter players of both teams evenly all over the playing area. Toss in a soccer ball and watch the fun. The effect is like a giant pinball machine.

PASS IT ON

The entire group forms a circle. Everyone is given an object that can be large, small, or any shape (a bowling ball, a trash can, a shoe, etc.). At a signal, everyone passes his object to the person on his right, keeping the objects moving at all times. When a person drops any object, he is out, but his object remains in. As the game progresses, more people leave the game, making it harder and harder to avoid dropping an object because there becomes more objects than people very quickly. The winner is the last person(s) to drop out.

PING-PONG BASKETBALL

Have contestants bounce, at least one time (no limit otherwise), Ping-Pong balls into different size containers. Vary the amount of points given, for example the smaller the container, the larger the amount of points assigned.

PING-PONG BASEBALL

You can play a very exciting game of baseball indoors using Ping-Pong balls and Ping-Pong paddles. It requires a lot of room and is fast-moving. If the ball hits the ceiling on the fly, it is playable, but the walls are foul territory. All other baseball rules apply.

PING-PONG HOCKEY

A great way to play hockey in a small, confined area is to have teams get down on all fours and place a Ping-Pong ball in the center. The team must then blow the Ping-Pong ball through their goals (a doorway or the legs of a chair, etc.) without touching the ball. No goalies are used. If the ball touches a player, he goes to the penalty box. Two balls at once can make the game even more exciting.

PING-PONG POLO

For this exciting indoor game, have team members make their own polo sticks out of rolled-up newspaper and masking tape. (Several sheets of paper should be rolled up lengthwise and then taped along the edge.)

The object of the game is for team members to knock the ball (a Ping-Pong ball) with the polo stick into their team's goal. An excellent way to set up goals is to lay two tables on their sides (one table per goal) with the top of the table facing into the playing area. When the ball hits the face of the table, it will make a popping noise, indicating that a goal was scored. Each team should have one goalie who will guard the table. The goalie can use any part of his body to protect the table.

To make the game even more like real polo, have the kids ride horses (broomsticks) while they play the game. It's always advisable to have a few extra Ping-pong balls on hand.

PING-PONG TABLE BASEBALL

Here's a good indoor game for small groups. To set it up, you'll need a card table, a Ping-Pong ball, and some masking tape (for lines).

On the card table, mark off lines according to the diagram pictured below. You need foul lines and lines that indicate a base hit, a double, and a triple.

To play, place the Ping-Pong ball on home plate. The team at bat rotates and attempts to blow the ball across the bases for a home run. The team in the field places three players on their knees on the opposite side of the table who attempt to blow the ball off the table before a base hit is scored.

Here are some additional rules:

1. The batter may blow only once.
2. The fielders may not touch the table at any time.
3. If the ball crosses the foul lines, that player is allowed another blow, even if it was the fielding team that blew the ball back across the foul lines.

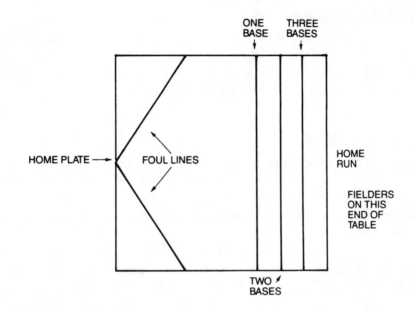

4. A ball's score is calculated at the point where it makes its farthest forward progress before being blown off the table toward the foul lines. For example, if the batter blows the ball and it reaches the third base tape before being blown off the table, the batter is credited with a triple. The next batter may get a double, putting two people on base—one on second and the previous batter on third. The next batter may hit a home run that would score three runs. Runs may only be forced in.
5. Outs are made by blowing the ball off the table before it reaches the first base line, so it does not go back across the foul line.
6. Home runs are made by blowing the ball off the table on the opposite end from home plate, for whatever reason. Fielders need to be careful about where they're blowing the balls; they can unintentionally score for the opposing team.

PYRAMID RACES

Divide into teams of six. Have each team build a three-level pyramid on the starting line. Then have the pyramids race. The three people on the bottom must travel while those on top must keep their balance. If the pyramid collapses, they must stop and rebuild it before continuing.

QUICK DRAW

This game is a fun way to play art charades. Divide into teams and have each team get as far away from each other as possible (in four corners of the room). The leader is in the center of the room and holds two boxes (one for each team) containing about twenty words or phrases on little slips of paper.

When the game begins, one member from each team runs to the center, takes a slip of paper out of their team's box, reads it, and gives it to the leader who discards it. The player then runs back to his team, picks up a drawing pad and a marking pen, and tries to draw the word or phrase. No letters or words are allowed, only pictures. The team tries to guess the word or phrase by looking at the drawing. The artist may not speak until someone finally guesses correctly.

As soon as the word or phrase is guessed, the next player runs to the leader and draws another slip of paper. Play continues until one team finishes all twenty.

The twenty words and phrases should be the same for all teams. Also, it might be wise to have an adult referee with each team. In that case, each contestant should bring the slip of paper to his team referee, so he knows what the phrase is and can determine when it is guessed.

RATTLESNAKE

For this game of stealth and skill, you will need two blindfolds, a small plastic bottle (a Rx bottle works fine) with a rock in it, and a defined area for play. This can be done on large mats (the wrestling-type) or on a carpeted floor. The referee blindfolds both people. One player is designated the rattlesnake; another the hunter. The hunter is spun in circles several times. It is essential that everyone remains absolutely quiet (everyone not playing is seated around the edges of the playing area). The referee says, "Rattlesnake." The rattlesnake must shake his rattler and then try to escape capture by the hunter. The game continues with the referee periodically saying, "Rattlesnake" until the hunter captures the rattlesnake.

ROLLER BASKETBALL

Using an outdoor basketball court, two teams on roller skates attempt to score points by hitting the opponent's backboard with a beach ball. (Teams can have between five to ten players each.) Players may either carry the ball or tap it, as in volleyball. If a player is tagged by an opponent while carrying the ball, the ball goes to the other team. The ball is put in play by a player passing it from out-of-bounds. A roughness penalty gives the opposing team a free throw from the basketball free throw line.

SANCTUARY SOCCER

This version of soccer allows you to play indoors and has a built-in equalizer to keep one team from dominating the game.

Play in a large room with all the chairs removed. You will need a Nerf soccer ball (or any soft ball) and eight folding chairs. Line up four chairs at each end of the playing area for goals. Play regular soccer, with as many players as you wish. A goal is scored when the soccer ball hits one of the other team's chairs.

When points are scored, the chair that is hit is removed from the goal of the team that was scored upon and added to the goal of the team who scored. Before the first goal is scored, the setup would look like this:

After team "B" scores a goal, the setup would look like this:

As a result, the team that was just scored upon will have an easier, larger target when the ball is back in play, while the other team has a smaller, more difficult target. Each team can have one goalie, as in regular soccer.

SCOOP

Have the group sit in a circle. You will need a round cookie tin lid, coin, or some other flat disc that can be spun on the floor. Everyone in the circle numbers off, and one person is chosen to be IT. IT spins the lid on its edge in the middle of the circle and calls a number. The lid must keep spinning long enough for IT to take a seat in the circle. Meanwhile, the person whose number was called jumps up and tries to pick up the lid with one hand before it falls over. If he is successful, the original IT comes back to the center and does it again. If not, the person whose number was called remains in the center as the new IT.

SHOE SHUCKING RACE

Divide into groups of six (girls must wear slacks). Each team member must lie on his back with his feet in the air, meeting in the center of the circle. A container of water (dishpan) is placed on the elevated feet. The object is for each member to remove his shoes without spilling his water. The team to win is the one with the most shoes off after three minutes.

SHOOT THE DUCK

This game can be played with any size group from six to sixty. The leader should have everyone assemble in one large circle with all the players facing in the same direction. Each one in the circle should then put his hand on the shoulder of the person ahead of him. Several leaders (or young people) depending on the size of the group should stand facing the players inside the circle, armed with loaded squirt guns. When the music begins, the group as a unit moves in its circle until the music stops. (You may use a whistle as a signal, too.) When the music stops, the player (duck) immediately in front of each of the armed leaders is shot with the squirt gun, like a sitting duck, and leaves the game. Play continues until the last duck left is declared the winner. (As more and more participants leave the game, the leader might want to decrease the number of shooters.) This game is exciting, and the tension runs high.

SHUFFLE YOUR BUNS

Here's a wild game you can play over and over again. Arrange chairs in a circle, so everyone has a chair. There should be two extra chairs in the circle. Each person sits in a chair, except for two people in the middle who try to sit in the two vacant chairs. The persons sitting in the chairs keep moving around from chair to chair to prevent the two in the middle from sitting down. If one or both of the two in the middle manage to sit in a chair, the person on their right replaces them in the middle of the circle and then tries to sit in an empty chair.

SOCKBALL

This is another version of baseball that is ideal for an indoor setting. Everything used in the game is made out of socks. Stuff a long tube sock full of socks to make a bat and make a ball the same way. Everyone must play in his stocking feet. On a freshly waxed gym floor, this game is really a riot.

SURPRISE MUSICAL CHAIRS

For this game, you will need chairs for everyone, many paper bags, and some balloons. Arrange the chairs for musical chairs, only there should be enough chairs for everyone. Blow up the balloons, put them inside the paper bags, close the bags, and place one on each chair. One of the sacks, however, contains a water balloon. The kids march around the chairs, and when the music stops (or at a signal), everyone sits down in a chair on top of the paper bag. Whoever sits on the water balloon is out. Leaders then rearm the chairs with more bags (make sure the kids aren't watching). Play continues until there is one player left. (You may have more, perhaps half, of the bags contain water balloons to save bags and to quicken the game.)

SWAT

The group sits in a circle, and in the center is a wastebasket turned upside down. One player is IT and stands inside the circle with a rolled-up newspaper. IT walks around the inside of the circle and swats one person's knee. IT must then put the newspaper back on top of the wastebasket and return to the swatted person's seat before that player grabs the newspaper and hits him back. If the newspaper falls off the wastebasket, IT must put it back.

TETHERBALL JUMP

For this game, have ten to twenty kids form a circle. You get in the center of the circle with a tethered ball (a ball attached to a rope about eight feet long). You take the rope in your hand and begin making circles with the ball, about six inches off the ground. The circle moves in closer, and each person must jump over the ball. You keep the ball going faster and faster until someone goofs and is eliminated. Whoever remains is the winner. As the game progresses, you can make the ball go faster and/or higher off the ground. (It is wise to have more than one ball twirler in case of dizziness.)

TOUCH

This game is easy to play and great indoors or outdoors. The kids first line up in some predetermined order (alphabetically, etc.). The leader shouts some object that everyone can see. All the kids run and touch it, then get back in their places in line. The last person to get back in line is out of the game. Any object can be used, including something that one person in line has, for example "Dick's right shoe." It's a wild game with a lot of activity.

TRAIN WRECK

This game is like "Fruitbasket Upset" (page 114). Arrange your chairs facing each other in two lines, with an aisle down the middle. Each person, including the conductor, is numbered and sits in a chair. The conductor stands in front and calls seven numbers (not his own). He then yells, "Train wreck!" The people with the numbers called must exchange seats with each other (it doesn't matter which seat as long as it's not your own). The conductor tries to find an empty seat. The person without a chair is the new conductor.

TRASH CAN BASKETBALL

This is an indoor version of basketball that can be played when the real thing is not available. Set up large trash cans at each end of the room. Use a soft ball about eight inches in diameter. Follow regular basketball rules with these exceptions:

1. There is no dribbling. All movement of the ball is by passing. This helps to make the game not only more practical but fairer in the coed situation.
2. There is no running with the ball, only passing to a teammate.
3. If you touch a player with the ball, that's a foul. The fouled player gets a free shot.
4. There should be a circle drawn around the trash cans about six feet from the cans, which is a no-man's land—no one is allowed here. This prevents goal tending and dunking, making the game fairer for everyone.

TRIPLE THREAT BASKETBALL

Here's another new way to play basketball. It requires one basket and three teams. You can have three teams of any size; however, a maximum of five players and a minimum of two would be best. The rules of the game are the same as for regular basketball, with these changes:

1. Baskets are worth one point. The game is played until one team has ten points and is leading the other two teams by at least two points each.

2. After each basket is scored, the team in last place is awarded the ball out-of-bounds, even if they were the team that just scored. In the event that two teams (or all three teams) are tied for last, the team that has had the low point total the longest is awarded the ball. (You may want to come up with some other system that seems fair.)

3. In the event that play is stopped for some reason other than a basket, such as the ball going out-of-bounds, traveling, double dribble, etc., the team in last place is again awarded the ball. If the last place team was guilty of the violation, the ball is given to the team next to last.

4. In the event of a foul, the team that was fouled takes the ball out-of-bounds—no foul shots.

This game can be played with two baskets on a regular basketball court. The teams rotate baskets after each goal is scored. Part of the fun is trying to remember which basket is yours. Another variation would be playing with four teams and four baskets on each side of a square, if you have baskets that can be moved. You could, of course, play the game with a Nerf ball and cardboard boxes or trash cans for baskets.

TRUE-FALSE SCRAMBLE

Here's an active game that can also be educational. You will need to compile a list of questions that can be answered "true" or "false." These can be Bible questions or general knowledge questions.

Divide your players into two teams seated across from each other in two rows (see diagram). At one end is an empty chair marked "true," and at the other end an empty chair marked "false." Players on each team should number off, so there are the same numbers on each team.

To play the game, the leader reads a question and then calls a number. The two players with that number (one from each team) jump up and try to sit in the chair that represents the correct answer to the question. The first to sit wins a point for his team. It's a wild game, especially if you throw in a few hard questions.

TRUST TAG

This is the usual game of tag, except that the players play in groups of two. One partner must wear a blindfold. His teammate guides him by keeping his hands on his blindfolded partner's waist and shouting directions. The object is for the blindfolded player to tag another blindfolded player. A variation to make this game even more difficult would be to have the teammate give his blindfolded partner directions *only* by pushing or pulling him around.

WINK

Chairs are arranged in a circle, facing inward. One boy stands behind each chair with his hands behind his back. Girls sit in the chairs, except for one chair that is left vacant. The boy behind that particular chair is IT. He must get a girl into that chair. He does this by winking at any one of the girls seated in the other chairs. She then tries to get out of her chair without being tagged by the boy behind her. If she is tagged, she must remain in her chair, and IT tries again, either by winking at another girl or the same one. If the girl winked at can get out of her chair without being tagged, she takes the chair in front of IT, and the boy with the vacant chair is now IT. Anyone who can avoid becoming IT is the winner. Halfway through the game, have the boys switch places with the girls.

6.

MIXERS

All of the games in this chapter are designed to help people interact and become better acquainted. They are great as a first game when you get people together for a party or game activity. There are a variety of mixers here: Some are for large groups, some are for small groups, but they can all be adapted to fit your needs.

ACCIDENT REPORT

Give each person a pencil and paper. At a signal, such as two pie pans crashing together, each player is to bump shoulders with someone close. After bumping, an accident report must be filled out with each other's name, address, phone number, grade, driver's license number, etc. This can be continued six or eight times throughout the night's activities, each time bumping someone new. This is a good mixer and also a sneaky way of compiling a calling and mailing list for visitors.

BACK SNATCHING

Pin a name onto each person's back (either phony names, middle names, or real names if the group doesn't know each other very well). When the signal is given, each player starts copying names of the other players; at the same time he tries to keep people from copying the name on his own back. The result is a lot of twisting and turning. At the end of a time limit, the player with the most names on his list is the winner.

BALLOON MIXER

This is not only a good mixer, but a good way to choose couples for a game like "Birdie on the Perch" (page 71) or any other game that requires couples. All the girls or half the group (whichever is best) get a piece of paper and a balloon. They write their names on the pieces of paper then put them inside the balloons, blow up the balloons, and tie them. All the balloons are placed in the middle of the room. At a signal, the boys or the other half of the group grab a balloon, pop it, read the name on the piece of paper inside, and try to locate the person whose name they have. The last couple to locate each other and sit down on the floor is the loser.

BOGGLE MIXER

Divide your young people into small groups. Each group's players list their first names in large letters on a single piece of paper with a uniform left margin:

Each group then tries to make as many words as possible from the combined letters in the names. For example, words could be three letters or more with bonus points for five letter words (1), six letter words (2), etc. Any combination of letters can be used as long as the letters are contingent to each other. Proper names and foreign words are not permissible. Set a three minute time limit.

CONFUSION

This is an excellent mixer for any occasion. To play, each person needs a game sheet similar to the one below. Pencils should also be provided.

You will need to make up your own list of tasks. Usually seven or eight are all you need for an exciting and active game that lasts five or ten minutes. The object is to complete each task as quickly as possible. The first person to finish is the winner. While the game is being played, there is plenty of organized "confusion" in the room.

---

1. Get ten different autographs on the back of this sheet (first, middle and last names).
2. Unlace someone's shoe, then lace it again and tie it. Have the person initial here: _____
3. Get a hair over six inches long from someone's head. (Let them remove it.) He initials here: _____
4. Get a girl to roll a somersault and sign her name here: _____
5. Have a guy do five push-ups for you and sign his name here: _____
6. Play RING AROUND THE ROSY with three other people and have them sign here: _____
7. Do twenty-five jumping jacks and have someone count them off for you. He initials here: _____
8. Say the Pledge of Allegiance as loudly as you can with two other people. One of them initials here: _____
9. Leap-frog over someone wearing white shoes. He initials here: _____

DUMB DOLORES

For a good way to acquaint a group, have all the kids sit in a circle. One kid gives his name plus an adjective that begins with the first letter of his name. Some examples: Barfy Bob, Happy Harry, Awful Alan, etc. The next kid repeats the first kid's goofy name and then gives his own the same way. The game continues around the circle with each kid having to remember everybody before him and then himself. The last guy has to name everybody. For a long time kids remember each other as "Weird Wayne" or "Beautiful Bill" or "Dumb Dolores." This game should be limited to thirty or less.

GETTING TO KNOW YOU

Give everyone in the group a copy of the chart below. Each person attempts to get someone to sign a box containing a description that truthfully describes him. The first person to get all the boxes signed, or after a reasonable time, the one with the most boxes signed wins. Someone can sign more than one box if more than one description truthfully describes him.

The winner then reads to the group the signers and the descriptions they signed under, which ends the game with laughter.

I feel like my breath is bad.	I am madly in love with someone in this room.	On a scale of ten, my sex appeal is about a three.	The last date I went on was real bad.
I have dandruff.	I am on a diet.	I am good looking but not conceited.	I want to be president of the U.S.
I have seriously considered trading my folks in on a new stereo.	Basically, my brother/sister is a turkey.	I am afraid of the dark.	I think school is a waste of time.
I don't like my voice. It's too high.	I have B.O. a lot.	I am going to be famous someday.	All of my teeth are not real.

GROUP UP

This game is similar to both "Barnyard" (page 69) and "Clumps" (page 77). The entire group mingles around the room, and the leader yells a characteristic, such as "First initial of first name." Everyone must quickly get into groups that have that characteristic. When the leader blows the whistle, the group with the most people in it is the winner.

Other possible characteristics are these:
1. Number of people in your immediate family
2. Month of birth
3. Favorite color
4. Color of shirt
5. Age
6. Grade in school
7. Community you live in

GUESS WHO

For an easy get-acquainted activity, ask each young person to write something about himself that probably no one else knows. If the kids have trouble coming up with a unique contribution, suggest an unusual pet they might have, a weird snack or sandwich, or if desperate, their mother's middle name. Collect all the responses.

Read the clues to the group and ask them to guess the person they think the clue identifies. Give one thousand points for each correct guess. Everyone keeps his own score. For a prize, give a copy of the church directory or an address book to write what they learned about people in the group.

IDENTITY

As your group enters the room, have them fill out name tags and drop them in a basket. After everyone has arrived, have them stand in a circle. Pass the bucket around and have each person take a name tag (not their own) without letting everyone else see the name.

Then have everyone turn to the left and place the name tag he is holding on the back of the person standing in front of him. The object of the game is to discover the name printed on the name tag pinned to your back. Identify the name by asking questions that can be answered "yes" or "no"—questions such as, "Do I have red hair?" or "Am I wearing jeans?" Each kid can ask only two questions to each person they meet.

When a person discovers whose name he has, he goes to that person, places his hands on that person's shoulders, and proceeds to follow him around the room. As more people discover their identity, the lines of people with hands on shoulders will lengthen until the last person finds his identity.

Another way to play this game is to use stickers (adhesive labels) rather than name tags. Then, rather than putting them on each other's backs, they are placed on each others' *foreheads*. This makes it possible to talk to someone while looking at the name they have on their forehead.

HUMAN BINGO

Here is a fun way to break the ice and learn everybody's name. Give each person a bingo card (see the sample below). Fill in the squares with the names of people who fit the various descriptions. Each person must sign his own name. The first person to complete five blocks in a row yells bingo.

INTERROGATION

This is an especially good game to get better acquainted with new people in the group or with the sponsors.

Someone with a pimple	Someone who owns a dog	Someone who is wearing contact lenses	A foreign student	Someone who owns a motorcycle
Someone with three brothers	Someone who is going bald	Someone with red hair	Someone who got an "A" in English	Someone who just ate at McDonald's
Someone with blond hair at least twelve inches long	An amateur photographer	Sign your own name	Someone who has been to Canada	Someone who weighs less than 100 pounds
Someone who plays football	Someone who likes to jog	Someone wearing blue socks	Someone who drives an imported car	Someone who owns a horse
Someone born out of the U.S.	Someone who can play a guitar	Someone who had a bad date over the weekend	Someone who has a cowboy hat	Someone who weighs over 200 pounds

Begin by dividing into any number of teams. Each team gets a person to interrogate. The groups are told that the leaders have prepared a list of twenty questions, such as "What is your favorite food?" or "When is your birthday?" The group, however, doesn't know what those questions are. They have ten minutes to interrogate their person and try to get as much information as possible. When the time is up, they are given the questions and must try to answer them as best they can. If they have done a good job of interrogating their person, then they will be able to answer most of the questions. The team that answers the most questions correctly is the winner.

I'VE GOT YOUR NUMBER

As kids arrive, they each get a number that they must wear in a conspicuous place. Ahead of time, prepare lots of instructions (see the instructions below) on little slips of paper that are placed in a box.

Borrow something from #1.

Introduce #2 to #7.

Have #6 get you a glass of water.

Find out #12's middle name.

When everyone has his number, kids each take a slip of paper with an instruction on it. When they have completed the instructions, they come back and get new ones. At the end of a time limit (5 minutes or so), whoever has completed the most instructions wins. Make sure you make plenty of instructions.

JOHN-JOHN

This game is a great mixer for a large group.

Everyone forms a circle and faces in, except for a few people (the number depends on the number of players) who stand in the middle. On "go," the people in the middle each run up to a person of the opposite sex in the circle, put their hands on their hips, and shout, "What's your name?" to that person who shouts his name (for example, "Donna!"). The person in the middle shouts, "Donna!" over his shoulder and does a little dance (similar to the Mexican Hat Dance). For example, "Donna! . . . Donna! . . . Donna Donna Donna!" (he shouts the name as he dances).

After dancing, he turns around (his back to Donna), and Donna grabs onto his waist (like forming a train). Together they run across the circle to the other side, and the first person again goes up to a person of the opposite sex, puts his hand on his hips (so does Donna), and he shouts, "What's your name?" She says her name, and both he and Donna shout the name over their shoulders one-at-a-time and do the little dance together. Then they both do an about-face, and the new person hooks on. The chain now has the first person in the middle, Donna in front, and the new person in the rear. They run across the circle as the game continues.

The object is to see which chain can get the longest by the time everyone has been included in one. Once chains cannot find people of the opposite sex, they can run up to anyone. With groups of several hundred, the chains can get very long and usually collide, adding to the excitement of the game.

LET'S GET ACQUAINTED

A list similar to the one below should be printed and given to each person in the group who is to fill in all the blanks with someone's name who fits the description. The first person to get all his blanks completed or the one who has the most at the end of the time limit is the winner. Be creative in making lists to fit your own group to help kids get to know each other a little better.

LET'S GET ACQUAINTED

1. Find someone who uses Listerine _____
2. Find someone who has three bathrooms in his house _____
3. Find someone who has gotten more than two traffic tickets _____
4. Find someone who has red hair _____
5. Find someone who gets yelled at for spending too much time in the bathroom
6. Find someone who has been inside the cockpit of an airplane _____
7. Find someone who plays a guitar _____
8. Find someone who likes to eat frog legs _____
9. Find someone who has been to Hawaii _____
10. Find someone who uses your brand of toothpaste _____
11. Find someone who has used an outhouse _____
12. Find a girl with false eyelashes on _____
13. Find a guy who has gone water skiing and got up the first time _____
14. Find someone who knows what "charisma" means _____
15. Find someone who is on a diet _____
16. Find a girl who uses a Lady Remington Shaver _____
17. Find a guy who has a match with him _____
18. Find someone who has his own private bath at home _____
19. Find someone who doesn't know your last name _____
20. Find someone who has a funny sounding last name _____

MATCH MIXER

This is a great way to help kids in a youth group get to know each other better. Give each person three 3 X 5 cards (or slips of paper). Everyone writes something about himself on each card. Suggested topics could be these:

1. The most embarrassing thing that ever happened to me
2. My secret ambition
3. The person I admire most
4. My biggest hang-up
5. If I had a million dollars, I would. . .

All the cards are collected and redistributed three to each person. No one should have his own card. At a signal, everyone tries to match each card with a person in the room by asking questions to determine whose card he has. Whoever matchs the three cards first is the winner. All the kids finish and then share their findings with the rest of the group.

MATCH-UP

Here's a good game that can be used as an ice breaker or mixer. It really gets people talking with each other and is a lot of fun. Index cards are typed or written with statements like those listed below. The words in italics are typed onto the right-hand portion of the card that is then cut off (see illustration).

Here is a sample list of phrases:

I always eat bacon with *my eggs.*

Tarzan lived in the jungle with his wife *Jane.*

The worth of the American dollar is about *40 cents.*

We could save on gasoline with fewer *jack-rabbit starts.*

To get a mule's attention, you must first hit him with *a board.*

What good is a peanut butter sandwich without *peanut butter?*

Speak softly and carry a big *stick.*

The large and small portions of the cards are handed out randomly to people with the instructions that they are to find the correct match-up with their portions. They must do this by introducing themselves to someone, then holding their cards together and reading them out loud. Some combinations can be very funny. If two people think they have a match, they must go to the designated leader and check them. If they have a correct match, they can sit down. Another variation is to give everyone one large and one small portion of cards that do not match and make them find a match for each portion (two matches total).

MONEY MAKER

This is a great mixer for crowds of twenty-five or more. Before the group assembles, slip a dollar bill to five participants (adjust the number to group size) and instruct them not to tell anyone they have it. On "go," the group moves around and shakes hands, introducing themselves and sharing any other pertinent information you specify. The people in the group who have dollar bills in their pockets will give them to the twentieth person (adjust to group size) who shakes their hand. Dollar-bill holders silently keep track of the count but holler when #20 shakes their hands. It's a guaranteed way to get the crowd excited and moving fast.

If this sounds too mercenary, make the prize something other than money or simply award points in the same fashion. Whoever has the most points at the end of the game wins. Either way, it really gets people interacting with each other.

NAME GUESS
On slips of paper write different names of famous people and pin one to the back of each person, not letting them see who they are. To help him guess who he is, each person asks other group members questions that can be answered "yes" or "no." The first person to guess correctly wins; the last person to guess correctly is the loser.

NAME SEARCH
This game helps people who don't know each other to become familiar with the names of everyone in the group. (Make sure there are no lists containing the names of the group anywhere.) Put a large name tag on each person.

```
K  E  U  S  O  L  D  X  N
A  L  L  A  N  A  R  F  V
T  T  O  K  R  S  J  A  D
H  T  E  B  A  Z  I  L  E
Y  R  G  G  L  T  Z  R  Y
R  E  T  E  P  P  L  A  K
M  I  J  K  H  L  R  A  C
T  R  S  H  A  R  O  N  W
```

Give each person a word search puzzle (see illustration) with every person's name somewhere in the puzzle. Of course, to do the puzzle people have to know the names they are looking for, which means they need to walk around and look at all the name tags.

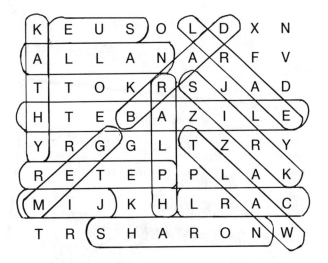

NAME TAG MIXER

Here's a good suggestion for a mixer when people do not know each other very well. Make name tags for each person that are about eight inches (or more) square. In the middle write the person's name but leave enough room on the name tag for other things to be written. When you are ready to begin, give each person *someone else's* name tag and have them find the person who belongs to it. After they have found that person, they can pin or hang the name tag on him. Once they have their own name tags, they continue going around the room meeting people and having each person autograph their name tags. After ten or fifteen minutes, stop and give a prize to whoever has the most names on his name tag.

NAME THAT PERSON

Here's a good, competitive game that helps kids get to know each other a lot better. Divide into two even teams. For larger groups, divide into four teams and have a play-off with the two winning teams and two losing teams.

Give each person a blank 3 X 5 card (or piece of paper) and have him write five little-known facts about himself (see examples below) and sign his name.

1. I have a pet snake
2. My middle name is Hortense
3. I was born in Mexico City
4. I hate pizza
5. The carpet in my bedroom is green   — Mike Johnson

Collect all the cards and keep separate stacks for each team. The game is now ready to play.

The object is to *name that person* on the card that the leader draws (from the other team's stack of cards) in as few clues as possible. Begin by opening up the bidding between the teams, for example "We can name that person in five clues!"; "We can name that person in four clues!"; etc. The team that wins the bidding has five seconds to guess after the reading of the appropriate number of clues. Appoint a spokesperson from each group and rotate. They can huddle together to come up with an answer. The more interaction between team members, the better. If they miss or if they don't respond in five seconds, the points go over to the other team. The scoring goes like this:

1 clue   = 5 points
2 clues = 4 points
3 clues = 3 points
4 clues = 2 points
5 clues = 1 point

Proceed with the game until every card has had one guess. Total up the points and announce the winner. Award prizes if you wish. Another variation of the game is to read the rest of the clues on the card after it has been played if they haven't yet been read and if the original guess was wrong. Then let them try to guess again—just for fun.

ODDBALL MIXER

Here's a good mixer for almost any size group. Before the game begins, have ten guys and ten girls prepare themselves to fit the descriptions on the list below and keep their descriptions as secretive as possible until the game begins. Then, give each person a list of the descriptions. You can use one list for everyone or you can prepare two separate ones— one for the guys and one for the girls. The first person to find the people who fit the descriptions and write in their names wins. You can make up your own descriptions to fit the people in your group.

FOR THE GIRLS, FIND THE BOY WHO . . .

1. Has a red comb in his back pocket. _____

2. Has a rubber band around his sock. _____

3. Has his wrist watch on upside down. _____

   4. Has his shoes on the wrong feet. _____

   5. Has a thumb tack in the heel of his right shoe. _____

   6. Has a bobby pin in his hair. _____

   7. Has a Band-Aid on his neck. _____

   8. Has his shoe laced from the top down. _____

   9. Has only one sock on. _____

  10. Has his belt on upside down. _____

FOR THE GUYS, FIND THE GIRL WHO. . .

   1. Has one earring on. _____

   2. Has a rubber band around her wrist. _____

   3. Has on mismatched earrings. _____

   4. Has a penny in her shoe. _____

   5. Has lipstick on her ear. _____

   6. Has a paper clip on her collar. _____

   7. Has nail polish on one fingernail. _____

   8. Has on one false eyelash. _____

   9. Is chewing bubble gum. _____

  10. Has on one nylon stocking. _____

SEVEN BEANS

This is a mixer that works best with a big crowd. Everyone is given seven beans. The kids walk around the room asking each other questions. Every time a the player gets another player to answer a question with a "Yes" or "No," he wins a bean from that player. The game continues for ten to fifteen minutes. The person with the most beans wins a prize.

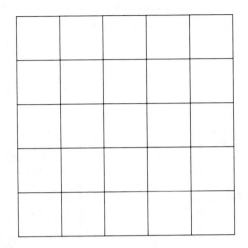

PEOPLE BINGO

Randomly select the names of enough people in your group to fill in each square on "Bingo People" playing cards, one name to a square (see illustration). Write them on slips of paper to be mixed in a hat. Give every player a blank playing card. Then they all look around the room and write somebody's name in each square. From a hat, draw the players' names. If a player has the announced name on his card, he marks an "X" through that name. Whoever has a row of "X's" either horizontally, vertically, or diagonally wins.

RATTLE TATTLE

Have your kids bring a dollar's worth of change and play this version of bingo. Give each person a game sheet (see illustration). Then have the group mingle and find people who have coins described on the sheet or who can answer the questions correctly. Five in a row—up, down, or diagonally—wins.

The game can also be played individually by allowing players to use only the coins in their possession to fill in the spaces. Adapt the rules to make it harder or easier, according to your situation.

A nickel minted between 1970 & 1975	A game token	A penny made before 1950	What does *E Pluribus Unum* mean?	A half dollar
Exactly 37¢ in change	A dime minted between 1981 & 1983	A quarter with a small "d" on it	What is the name of the building on the penny?	Four quarters
A quarter more than 25 years old	Whose picture is on the quarter?	A foreign coin	A nickel minted between 1951 & 1955	A 1983 penny
Seventeen pennies	Five dimes	Which president is on the dime?	Exactly 63¢ in change	A penny, a nickel, a dime, and a quarter
Six coins all the same	A silver dollar	No quarters	A 1972 quarter	Someone who can flip heads three times in a row

SIGNATURES

This is a mixer that can be used with any age group. It's easy and fun to play. Give each person a sheet of paper and a pencil. Written down the left-hand side of the paper are the letters in a word or phrase selected because of its association with the holiday or the occasion of the party. For example, at a Christmas party, the words written down the side might be "Merry Christmas."

At a signal, the players try to find someone whose first or last name begins with one of the letters in the key word or phrase. When someone is found, he is asked to sign next to the appropriate letter. The first person to get signatures next to all of the letters on his sheet is the winner. If there is no winner after a certain period of time, stop the game, and whoever has the most signatures is the winner. In case of a tie, whoever has the most first names that match wins. The phrase can be longer for large groups or shorter for small groups,

THE SITUATION GAME

If your group is sitting in a circle or in rows of chairs, here is a fun game to liven things up. Have everyone whisper to the person on their right, "You are . . . (Batman, Brigitte Bardot, etc.)." Be creative! To the person on their left, they whisper, "You are in . . . (in the bathtub, on top of a flagpole, etc.)." Next everybody finds new seats. Then they whisper to the person on their right, "You are wearing . . ." To the person on their left, they whisper, "You are doing ..." Now each person tells the group "who" he is, "where" he is, "what he is wearing," and "what he is doing." The results are hilarious.

STATISTICAL TREASURE HUNT

Here is an exceptionally good game to get groups acquainted. Divide your group into teams of equal number, if possible. Give each team a typewritten or mimeographed sheet of questions that are to be answered and evaluated as indicated on the sheet. Each team appoints a captain who acts as the gleaner of information and recorder. (This game can be played around tables at banquets.)

Below is a list of typical questions and methods of scoring. These may suggest other questions to you that may be more appropriate for your particular group or occasion.

General Questions:

_____ 1. Counting January as one point, February as two points and so on through the calendar year, total the number of birthday points at your table—only for months not years.

_____ 2. Counting one point for each different state named, total the score for the different number of birth states represented.

_____ 3. Total all the shoe sizes—one foot only.

_____ 4. Total the number of operations everyone at your table has had. Serious dental surgery counts, but not just an ordinary tooth pulling. Save all the interesting details for later!

_____ 5. Total your hair color score: Black counts two; brown counts one; blond counts three; red counts five; gray counts three; white counts five.

_____ 6. Score a point for each self-made article worn or carried by your teammates.

_____ 7. Add the total number of miles traveled by each member to get to this meeting.

_____ 8. Total the number of children teammates have. If husbands and wives are sitting together or are on one team, count their children only once. Score as follows: Each child counts one point; set of twins counts five points; grandchildren count three points each.

_____ 9. Score one point for each different college attended, but not necessarily graduated from.

STICKER MIXER

Here's a good get-acquainted activity for large groups. Write everyone's name on a sticker (pressure-sensitive round ones work best) and distribute them at random. Have everyone stick the label somewhere on his face. Then, each player tries to find his own name on someone else's face and sticks it on his own shirt. These two players stick together until the unstickered player finds his name. This is a good way for kids to see a lot of faces in a short time.

WHOPPER

This is a good game for groups that know each other fairly well. Give each person a piece of paper and pencil to write four things about himself—three must be true, and one must be a *whopper*, which is disguised to sound true. (Make the true statements little-known facts, so the whopper sounds true by comparison.)

Everyone reads his list, and each person tries to guess which statement is the whopper. (Don't reveal the whopper until everyone has guessed.) Whoever guesses correctly gets a point. The person whose list is being read gets a point for each incorrect guess.

A variation would be to guess which statement is true out of three whoppers.

7.

RELAYS

PLAY IT!

Relays are great *all-purpose* games that can be played indoors or outdoors, with large groups or small groups. They involve teamwork as well as individual competition.

All relays are basically the same: Teams line up and each team member must run the relay course or perform a particular task in succession. The first team to have all their members complete the relay is the winner.

Here is a basic relay game set-up, with four teams involved:

Returns to end of line

TEAM 1 ○ ○ ○ ○ ○ ○   ○   TEAM 1
                                                     GOAL

TEAM 2 ○ ○ ○ ○ ○ ○ - - → SAME AS ABOVE   ○   TEAM 2
                                                     GOAL

TEAM 3 ○ ○ ○ ○ ○ ○ - - → SAME AS ABOVE   ○   TEAM 3
                                                     GOAL

TEAM 4 ○ ○ ○ ○ ○ ○ - - → SAME AS ABOVE   ○   TEAM 4
                                                     GOAL

Here is another exciting way to run relays, which adds the possibility of a collision in the center of the playing area:

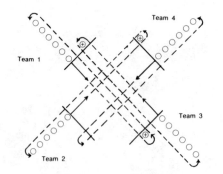

166

This chapter contains some of the best relay games ever created. They can, of course, be changed or adapted to fit your needs.

BACKBALL RELAY

This relay involves couples. A ball (like a basketball or volleyball) is placed between the two players, just above the belt line as the couple stands back-to-back. With their arms folded in front of them (not using their elbows), they must carry the ball around a chair (or some other goal) about thirty feet away.

BACK-TO-BACK RELAY

Again, this one requires couples who stand back-to-back. They are tied together with a short rope and must run to a goal and back, with one person running forward and the other running backward. On the return trip, the person who ran forward runs backward, and vice versa.

167

BALLOON BAT RELAY

Teams line up single file with the kids as close together as possible. Each team gets a balloon. The person at the front of the line bats the balloon with his hand between his legs, and each successive team member does the same until it reaches the last person. He runs it back to the front of the line, and the game continues until the team is back in its original order.

BALLOON POP RELAY

Each team member runs to a chair, blows up a balloon, and then sits on it until it pops.

BALLOON SWEEP RELAY

Players must maneuver a balloon around a goal and back using a broom, sweeping the balloon along the floor. It's not easy.

BASKETBALL PASS

Teams line up single file. The player in the front is given a basketball (or any other large ball). The first player passes it to the player behind him over his head. The next person passes it between his legs to the person behind him, and so on. The last person gets the ball, goes to the front of the line, and starts the whole process all over again. The first team to get back in its original order wins.

BAT ROUND RELAY

Each team gets a baseball bat that is placed on one end of the playing area, with the team lined up at the other end. Each player runs to the bat, puts his forehead on the bat (held in a vertical position), and runs around the bat ten times while still in that position. Then he must return to his team without falling down.

BLINDMAN CHARIOT RACES

Girls ride on the shoulders of the guys who are blindfolded. The girls shout directions to the guys as they run around an obstacle course.

BLOW CUP RELAY

Give each team a fifteen foot piece of string with a sliding paper cup on the string (see illustration).

The string is held taut, and the paper cup is placed at one end. The team lines up single file. At the signal, each player must blow the cup to the other end (with his hands behind his back) and then push it back to the start for the next player. The first team to finish wins.

BOTTLE FILL RELAY

Each team appoints one kid to lie on the floor a certain distance away with an empty pop or milk bottle held on his forehead. Each team member runs to that person with a nonbendable cup filled with water and tries to fill the bottle. The bottle should be large enough, so it takes quite a few cupsful to fill it. The first team to fill their bottle wins.

BOTTOMS UP RELAY

For this game, you should divide your group into teams of equal size and have each team line up behind their first player. At a signal, the last player fills a pop bottle with water, sticks his finger in the bottle, turns it upside down, and passes it. Each player uses only his thumb to keep the water in. The first player pours the water into an empty container, runs to the back of the line where he refills the pop bottle, and starts it down the line again. The first team to fill their empty container wins.

BROOM JUMP RELAY

Divide into teams. The first couple on each team is given a broom. On "go," the couple grab the ends of the broom and run back through their team, holding the broom just above the floor. Everyone in line jumps over the broom. When the couple reaches the end of the line, they pass the broom back to the front using hands only—no throwing. The first team to have their original couple heading the team again wins.

BROOM TWIST RELAY

Some twenty or thirty feet away, a team leader holds a broom. When the game begins, each player runs to his team leader, takes the broom, holds it against his chest with the broom end (the bristles) up in the air over his head. Looking up at the broom, the player must turn around as fast as possible ten times, while the leader counts the number of turns. Then the player hands the broom back to the leader, runs back to the team, and tags the next player. Players become very dizzy.

BUMPER BOX RELAY

For this relay, you need a large refrigerator box for each team. Each player stands with the box over his head and the open end at his feet.

At a signal, the players race to the opposite wall (or goal) and back while their team shouts directions to them from behind the starting line. For an added dimension to this game, decorate the boxes with wild colors, team names, or whatever.

CATERPILLAR RELAY

This is a good camp game. Have the kids bring their sleeping bags and line up in teams, relay-style. The first player in line gets into the sleeping bag headfirst and races to a certain place and back while the team shouts directions to him. The first team finished is the winner. A variation is to have the kids crawl in their sleeping bags (like a caterpillar), which is slower, but safer.

CHARIOT RACES—INDOOR VERSION

This relay needs to be played on a slick floor (like a gym floor). Set up a circular track and have the teams line up at a starting line.

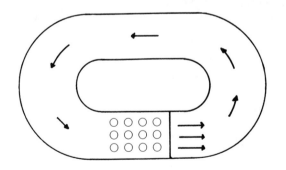

Have each team divide into threesomes—two horses and one rider.

(Usually it's best to have boys be the horses and girls be the riders.) The chariot is a blanket pulled by the horses, and the rider sits on the blanket, holding on for dear life. Each chariot must go around the track once, and then the next three players form a chariot, and so on.

CHARIOT RACES—OUTDOOR VERSION

This relay can be run the same as the previous one, but this time there is no blanket. The chariot is formed by having two boys face each other and lock their arms—right with right and left with left (crisscrossed arms). The rider (girl) sits on the boys' arms, and the boys race around the track (or a goal) and back.

A variation is to have four boys as the chariot and one girl rider. The four boys face the same direction in two rows of two. The girl rides up on their shoulders, with her hands on the shoulders of the two boys in front and her knees on the shoulders of the two boys in back. It's a wild game and a lot of fun.

COIN, BOOK, & BALL RELAY

This relay is fun to watch. Each team is given one quarter, one tennis ball (or any kind of ball that size), and a book. The idea is to balance the book on your head, hold the quarter in your eye, and keep the ball between your knees while walking to the finish line—no hands allowed.

COTTONBALL RACE

Provide each team with a number of cotton balls in a container, such as a dish or a pan. Each team also gets a spatula and an egg carton.

At a signal, the first person on each team picks up a cotton ball with a spatula and tries to keep it balanced on the spatula while running to a goal and back. If he loses the cotton ball, he must start over. When he returns to his team with the cotton ball, he puts it in the egg carton. The first team to fill their egg carton wins.

DRIVING THE PIGS TO MARKET
Line up the teams behind the starting line. Give the first player a wand (three foot stick, a yardstick, or a broom handle) and a pig (a coke bottle or egg). On "go," the first player drives the pig to the goal and back by pushing with his wand.

EGG-AND-ARMPIT RELAY
Half of the team lines up on each side of the room. The first person races to the other side with a spoon in his mouth and an egg on it. The teammate on the other side of the room takes the egg and puts it in his armpit and runs back across the room. He drops the egg from his armpit onto the next person's spoon.

EGG-AND-SPOON RELAY
Each player on each team gets a spoon. The teams line up, and a dozen eggs are placed on one end of the line. The players pass the eggs down the line using *only* the spoons—no hands, except for the first player putting the spoon on the egg. The winning team is the one that gets the most unbroken eggs down the line in the fastest time. A variation is to use marbles, instead of eggs.

EGG ROLL
In this relay, players roll a raw egg along an obstacle course with their noses. If the egg breaks, the player must start over with a fresh egg.

ELASTIC BAND RELAY

For this game, you will need to make several large circles out of elastic strips. Get some elastic strips about thirty-six inches long, overlap them

one inch, and stitch them on a sewing machine. The result will be several giant rubber bands.

This relay is simple. Each player runs to where the elastic band is lying, and puts his entire body through the band (over his head and down to his feet or vice versa), drops the band, and return to his team.

Round two can be two people doing it at once.

FAN THE BALLOON

Each team gets a balloon and a fan (anything such as a record album cover). At the signal, each player, without touching the balloon, must fan it around a goal and back, without the balloon touching the floor.

FEATHER RELAY

Give each team a box of small feathers (mallard or duck breast feathers work best). There should be one feather for each member of the team. At a signal, the first person on the team blows his feather (through the air) the length of the room and into a small box. At no time may he touch the feather. He may, on the other hand, blow an opponent's feather in the opposite direction, if the opportunity arises. The race continues until all the team has blown their feathers one-at-a-time into the box. This race can be doubly exciting if done on hands and knees.

FILL THE BOTTLE RELAY

One boy on each team puts a pop bottle in his back pocket. The rest of the team gets small paper cups. Team members dip water out of a pail, run to the boy with the bottle in his pocket, and attempt to fill the bottle. The first team to succeed is the winner.

FOREHEAD RELAY

This relay is for couples on a team. Each couple races to a goal and back while carrying a grapefruit or balloon between their foreheads. If it is dropped, they must start over.

FRISBEE RELAY

This is a good outdoor relay. Divide the group into equally-sized teams of five or six and give each team a Frisbee. Any number of teams may play at once. The playing area should have plenty of length, such as a road or a large open field. Each team should spread out in a line with players about fifty feet or more apart. The first person throws the Frisbee to the second, who allows the Frisbee to land. Then that person stands where the Frisbee landed and throws it toward the third person, who throws it to the fourth, and so on. The object is to see which team can throw it the greatest distance in the shortest time. Award points for throwing it the farthest and for finishing first.

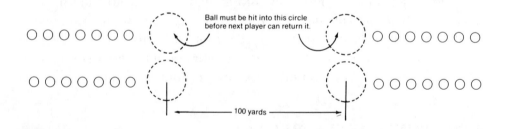

Ball must be hit into this circle before next player can return it.

100 yards

GOLFENNIS

This is actually a golf game using tennis balls, instead of regular golf balls. Provide the kids with plenty of tennis balls, golf clubs (7 irons work best), and an open space (a golf course or a football field). For this relay race, line up the teams, with half the team at one end of the playing area and the other half at the other end about one hundred yards away (see diagram). The first person hits the ball to the first person on the other half of his team as quickly as possible, then that person returns it, and so on. The first team to have all their players hit the ball wins. It's a lot of fun because when you are in a hurry, a tennis ball hit by a golf club can go anywhere.

GOTCHA RELAY

Divide the group into two teams. Set up the room or field similar to the diagram below. Each team lines up single file behind their markers. On "go," the first players run around the track like a regular relay race for one lap and tag the next players.

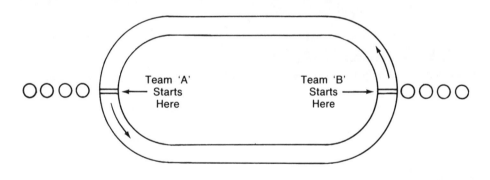

The object is to tag the runner of the other team. The teams continue to run the laps until a person is finally caught (Gotcha!).The team that catches the other first is the winner. Be sure to divide the teams so they are about even in speed. A variation is to run piggyback, on tricycles, or hopping on one foot.

✳ GRAB BAG RELAY

Teams line up single file behind a line. A paper bag containing individually wrapped edible items is placed on a chair at the opposite end of the room. At a signal, the first person in line runs to the chair, sits down, reaches into the bag without looking, pulls out an item, unwraps it, and eats it. When he has swallowed the last bite, an official okays it, and he runs back to the starting position, and the next player takes his turn. Each player must eat whatever he grabs out of the bag. The first team to eat all the contents of the grab bag wins. Suggestions for the grab bag are pickles, olives, cereal, onions, candy, and carrots.

GRAPEFRUIT PASS

This is a good coed relay game. Teams line up boy-girl-boy-girl. A grapefruit is started at one end of the line and passed under the chins of the players—no hands. If dropped, the grapefruit must be started at the front of the line again.

GREAT CHICKEN RACE

This is a relay where couples participate. The girl jumps on the back of a blindfolded guy and runs him through an obstacle course by giving him directions, but she is handicapped by having a raw egg in her mouth. If she breaks it, both are a mess.

GUZZLE RELAY

Each person gets a drinking straw. A gallon of apple cider (or some other beverage) is placed a certain distance away. When the whistle is blown, the first person in line runs to the cider and starts guzzling. When the whistle blows again, he stops and the next person takes over. (Some people get a short drink, others a long drink, depending on your best judgment.) The first team to finish their gallon of cider wins.

HANDSFUL RELAY

Use your imagination to collect an interesting variety of at least twelve identical pairs of items (two brooms, two balls, two skillets, two rolls of bathroom tissue, two ladders, etc.) Set up two tables and place one item from each pair on each table.

Line up a team for each table. The first player runs to his table, picks up one item of his choice, runs back to his team, and passes it to the second player. The second player carries the first item back to the table, picks up another item, and carries both items back to the third player. Each succeeding player carries the items collected by his teammates to the table, picks up one new item, and carries them all back to the next player. The game will begin rapidly but will become slower as each player decides which item to add and then passes his armload of items to the next player.

Once picked up, an item cannot touch the table or floor. Any item dropped in transit or transfer must be returned to the table by the leader. No one may assist the giving and receiving players in their exchange, except through coaching. The first team to empty their table wins.

HULA HOOPLA

Here are a few good relays using the famous hula hoop, which is still available in most toy stores.

1. Place a hula hoop on the floor twenty or more feet in front of each team. The object is for each player to run to the hoop, pick it up and "hula" five or ten times (you decide how many), drop it, and return to the line.

2. Have each player "hula" while walking or running to a goal twenty or more feet from the team and "hula" back. If the hula hoop drops, the player must stop, get the hoop going again, and continue.

3. Place the hoop twenty or more feet from the team. The player

runs to the hoop, stands in the hoop, and works it up and over his head with just his feet, legs, arms, etc.—no hands.

4. This relay is similar to the one above only two or three people run to the hoop at the same time, and without hands, work the hoop up around their waists. Then they run to a goal and back with the hoop in place around their waists—no hands.

HUMAN OBSTACLE COURSE

For this relay, each team lines up single file behind a starting line. Ten additional team members are used as the obstacle course: a standing pole to circle around, a leg tunnel to go under, kneelers on all fours to leap over, sitters with outstretched legs to step in and among, another standing pole to circle around and back to the starting line. At the signal, the first person runs the course, then the next person, and so on. If an obstacle is missed or improperly executed, the runner must repeat that obstacle.

INNER-TUBE RELAY

Teams divide into couples (same sex or opposite sex—you decide) and line up in different corners of the room. One inner tube (regular auto tire size) for each team is placed in the center of the room. Each couple must run to the inner tube, put it over their heads, and squeeze through the tube together. The first team to have all its couples finish wins.

INNER-TUBE-ROLL RELAY

Divide the group into teams with an even number of people on each team. Ask each team to pair up. The first couple from each team stands behind the starting line. A large inflated inner tube (preferably a bus or truck tire size) is placed on the floor between them. Before the game begins, make certain the players understand they cannot touch the inner tube with their hands. At the whistle, the couple must stand the tube up and together roll it around a chair and back to the starting line. If the inner tube falls while they are rolling it, they must come back to the starting line and begin again. When the couple successfully completes their round trip, the next couple places the tube flat on the floor, and without using their hands, shand it up and repeat the process.

IRON MAN RELAY

This relay involves six steps. Teams line up in a single-file line about fifteen feet from a basketball goal (or at the foul line on a basketball court). At the signal, the first two people leapfrog to a designated spot. At the point the first guy in line gets a peanut and rolls it with his nose to another designated spot while the second guy goes back to the front of the line. After rolling the peanut, he then takes a spoon and puts a Ping-Pong ball in it and walks to another designated spot. There he gets a basketball and goes to the back of the line. He then rolls the basketball through the entire team's legs and runs to the front of the line to retrieve it. When he successfully catches the basketball, he makes a basket. After making a basket, he then drinks a small glass of coke and burps, and the next two people continue the game. The winning team is the one that has every member participate fully in each event and finishes first.

LEMON RELAY

Teams line up in straight lines. The first person is given a pencil and a lemon. The object is to push the lemon to the finish line and back, using only the pencil. The player must start over again if the lemon rolls out of the assigned lane. Stopping the lemon from rolling too far, too fast, makes this relay difficult.

LIFESAVER RELAY

Give each player a toothpick to hold in his teeth. The leader places a lifesaver on the toothpick of the players at the head of each line. It is then passed from toothpick to toothpick until it reaches the end of the line. If it is dropped before it reaches the end of the line, it must be started all over again. The winning team is the one whose lifesaver reaches the end of the line first.

MAD RELAY

In this relay, each player does something different. At the beginning of the race, each team is lined up single file. At a signal, the first person on each team runs to the other end of the course to a chair. On the chair is a bag containing instructions written on separate pieces of paper. The player draws one of the instructions, reads it, and follows it as quickly as possible. Before returning to the team, the player must tag the chair and then run back and tag the next runner. The team that uses all of its instructions first is the winner. Here are a few sample directions:

1. Run around the chair five times while continuously yelling, "The British are coming, the British are coming."

2. Run to the nearest person on another team and scratch his head.

3. Run to the nearest adult in the room and whisper, "You're no spring chicken."

4. Stand on one foot while holding the other in your hand, tilt your head back, and count, "10, 9, 8, 7, 6, 5, 4, 3, 2, 1, Blast off!"

5. Take your shoes off, put them on the wrong feet, and then tag your nearest opponent.

6. Sit on the floor, cross your legs, and sing the following: "Mary had a little lamb, little lamb, little lamb, Mary had a little lamb, its fleece was white as snow."

7. Go to the last person on your team and make three different funny-face expressions, then return to the chair before tagging your next runner.

8. Put your hands over your eyes and snort like a pig five times and meow like a cat five times.

9. Sit in the chair, fold your arms, and laugh hard and loud for five seconds.

10. Run around the chair backward five times while clapping your hands.

11. Go to a blonde and keep asking, "Do blondes really have more fun?" until he answers.

12. Run to someone not on your team and kiss his hand and gently pinch his cheek.

MATTRESS RELAY

This game is excellent for camps or large groups. The group is divided into two teams. The boys lie flat on their backs on the floor, side by side, alternating head to foot.

One girl is transported over the line of boys on a mattress and jumps off at the end. The mattress is then passed back, and another girl gets on. If any girl falls off, she must get back on the mattress where she fell off. The team of boys who transport their girls in the quickest time wins.

This works best when the boys are mostly senior high and when they use only fifteen girls—the lighter the girls, the better.

MATTRESS RACE

In this relay, the boys carry all the girls one-at-a-time a distance of one hundred feet on a mattress. The mattress must be carried shoulder high or the team has to start over. The first team to get all their girls across the finish line is the winner.

MARBLE SUCKING RELAY

Divide your group into several teams. Give each person a plastic straw and a paper cup. The first person on each team gets a marble in his cup. The object is to suck the marble up with the straw and drop it into the next person's cup. If the marble drops on the floor, the team must start over at the beginning. The first team to get the marble to the last person wins.

MESSAGE RELAY

Teams divide in half and stand a distance away from each other. Type out a crazy message on a piece of paper (one for each team) and give it to the first player who opens it, reads it, wads it up, and throws it on the ground. He runs to the next person at the other side and whispers it in his ear. Then that player runs back and tells it to the next player and so on until the last player runs to the leader and whispers it to him. The team who repeats the message closest to the original wins. Accuracy, not time, is most important, but the players must run. Here's a sample message: "Mrs. Sarah Sahara sells extraordinary information to very enterprising executives."

MONOCLE RELAY

In this relay, the first person in line puts a quarter in his eye (monocle-style) and holds it there, without using his hands, while running around a goal and back. If the quarter is dropped, the player must start over.

NEWS RELAY

Teams line up on one end of the room. On the other end, hang the front page of the newspaper, several clippings, or a whole newspaper. Ahead of time prepare questions about the news stories. Ask the questions, then one person from each team runs to the newspaper and locates the correct answer. The first player to shout it out wins for his team.

PAPER CHASE

Each person is given two pieces of paper (newspaper works fine), and he travels between two points stepping only on these papers. He steps on the paper in front of him, then turns around and picks up the one behind him, and places it in front of him, steps on it, and turns around and picks up the paper behind him, puts it in front of him, steps on it, and so on.

PEANUT BUTTER RELAY

The first person in line gets a glob of peanut butter on the end of his nose. After running around the team once (or around a goal), he passes the glob to the next person's nose without using any hands, and so on. The object is not only to be the first to finish but also to be the team with the largest glob of peanut butter on the last person's nose.

PEANUT SWEEP RELAY

Have two teams line up in a shuttle formation (one half of the team lines up single file behind a line; the other half lines up behind a second line facing them). The first person on each team is given a broom (children's broom or regular). A small pile of peanuts is piled in front of him. At the whistle, the person with the broom sweeps peanuts to the opposite line and gives the broom to the first person in that line. This person in turn sweeps the peanuts back to the other line and so on until all the people in both lines have taken their turns. The first team finished wins.

PING-PONG BALL RELAY

Select several kids to race Ping-Pong balls. Each player gets a party blower (the type that uncoils when you blow it), and he is to push the balls across the floor using *only* those blowers. He cannot blow directly on the ball or touch it in any way escept with the party blower. First across the finish line wins.

POPPING PAIRS

This crazy relay is as much fun to watch as to play and works well with large groups. All you need is a large box of penny balloons and several *clean* inner tubes.

186

Divide your group into several equal teams of twenty or more. Have team members pair up in small groups of two each. Line the teams up behind a start/finish line. Make a pile of balloons for each team (one balloon for each team member in the pile). Place the piles of balloons (one pile for each team) fifty feet or more from the start/finish.

Instruct each pair to run to their pile of balloons where each one picks up a balloon, blows it up, and pops it with his foot before they return to tag the next pair on their team. However, each pair must position themselves back-to-back with an inner tube around them at their waists to run this relay. The first team to get all its members back across the start/finish line is declared the winning team. For added variety, use two inner tubes per pair instead of just one.

PORKY MALLOW

This game gets more difficult and funnier as it's played. Divide your group into two or more teams. Give each player a toothpick (round ones work best) and a marshmallow. The first player puts the marshmallow on his toothpick and then holds the toothpick with his teeth.

Pass the marshmallow from player to player *only* by sticking your toothpick into the marshmallow and leaving it as you pass it along—no hands allowed. As the marshmallow is passed, it accumulates one more toothpick from each player.

It's a riot to see players trying to avoid being stuck by the other toothpicks already in the marshmallow. The first team to finish is the winner. And the end product is a marshmallow that looks like a porcupine.

POTATO RELAY
Teams line up, and each player must push the potato along the floor to a goal and back, using *only* their noses. No hands are allowed.

ROLLERSKATE RELAY
Get a couple of pair of skates (preferably the kind that clamp onto your street shoes). Give each team a pair of skates and a skate key. Each team member must put on the skates and skate around a goal and return. It's a riot to watch.

SACK RACE
It's an oldie but goodie, but still a lot of fun. Get some old burlap bags (or pillow cases) and have kids race with their feet inside them, hopping to the goal and back.

SHOE BOX RELAY
Give each team one or more ordinary shoe boxes. If you have enough, give one to each player. Players then put their feet in the boxes and hoof it around the goal and back. It's fun to watch.

SHOE GRAB RELAY ✳

This is a great relay game for parties or big group get-togethers (the bigger the group, the better). First, everyone needs to take off his shoes and put them in a big pile at one end of the room (shoes should be as mixed up as possible). Next divide the group into even teams. On "go," the first person describes his shoes to the next person in line, who runs to the pile of shoes, finds the shoes, brings them back, and puts them on the first person. If the shoes are the wrong ones, he goes back and gets the right ones. The game continues with the last person in line describing his shoes to the first person. The team who has all their shoes on first is the winning team. This game is especially fun since so many kids wear similar shoes, making it almost impossible in some cases to find the right ones.

SKIPROPE-ISSY-DISSY RELAY

Each member of the team skips rope from a starting line to a goal where he lays down the rope and picks up a bat. He puts the small end of the bat to his forehead and with the large end on the ground spins around five times. He then picks up the skip rope and attempts to skip back to the starting line.

SKI RELAY

Construct skis out of plywood and nail old shoes (from the Goodwill or Salvation Army) to them. Divide your group into teams, and each member of the team wears skis to ski (walk, run, or . . . ?) to a pole, go around it, and return. Walking with the skis is a riot to watch, and going around the pole is really hard with long skis.

SKI TEAM RELAY

Make some skis out of plywood that will accommodate several team members at once. You can use old shoes, as described in the previous game, or you can use rope. (Just drill holes in the plywood and put the rope through the holes, forming loops for the players' feet.) Each team then races around a goal on these skis.

SOCK TAIL RELAY

Make several sock tails (a belt with a sock tied onto it that has an orange in the end of the sock), one for each team The first person on each team puts on that tail with the sock hanging down from his rear. Another orange is placed on the floor. At the signal, the player must push the orange on the floor to a goal and back with the sock tail. If he touches it with his feet or hands, he must start over. First team to have all members complete this task wins.

SUCKER RELAY

Teams line up. Each person has a paper straw. A piece of paper (about four inches square) is picked up by sucking on the straw and is carried around a goal and back. If the paper is dropped, the player starts over. First team to finish wins.

THIMBLE RELAY

The teams form a line, and each player has a straw that he holds upright in his mouth. The thimble is placed on the straw held by the first person in line. It is then passed from player to player by means of the straw. Whichever team gets the thimble to the end of the line first is the winner.

THREAD THE NEEDLE

Teams line up, and each gets a cold knife or spoon (just out of the freezer) with a long piece of string tied to it. The object is to be the first team to lace the entire team together by running the spoon through everyone's clothing—underneath clothes from the neck to the ankle. Each team member must keep advancing the string along as the spoon is being moved along, which requires a lot of teamwork.

THREE-LEGGED RACE

Here's another old favorite. Two players from each team stand side by side, and their two legs nearest each other are tied together. Then they race to the goal and back.

T.P. RELAY

Each team is given a roll of toilet paper. The team should be divided in half, with half the team on one end of the playing area and the other half on the opposite end. The first person in line puts the roll of toilet paper down on the ground and begins to unroll it by pushing it along with his nose. When he reaches the first person on the other half of the team, then that person turns the roll around and begins pushing it back, and so on until the entire roll is unrolled. The first team to finish unrolling is the winner.

WADDLE RELAY

In this relay, teams race with players carrying a small coin (penny or dime) between their knees. They must successfully drop the coin into a milk bottle or jar placed fifteen or twenty feet away, without using their hands. If the coin is dropped along the way, the player must start over.

WADDLE WALK RELAY

This one requires some real coordination, but anyone can do it. Players must walk to a goal and back with a balloon held between their knees and a cup of water balanced on their heads. If either the balloon breaks (or drops) or the cup of water falls off, the player must start over.

WAGON RELAY

For this one, you will need to obtain one or more wagons (the type that most kids have, but not too small). Each team pairs off—one person sits in the wagon and uses the handle to steer while the other person pushes him around a slalom course. When one couple finishes, the next begins, and the first team to have everyone complete the course wins.

A variation is to have one person ride in the wagon, just sitting there doing nothing, while the other person holds on to the handle and uses it both to steer and to push the wagon backward through the course. It's not easy.

WHEELBARROW RELAY

This is a variation of the old wheelbarrow race where Player A becomes the wheelbarrow by walking on his hands while Player B uses Player A's feet as handles and simply runs along behind. In this game, you do basically the same thing, but for added difficulty player A must push a volleyball along the ground with his nose.

WHEELBARROW EAT RELAY

This is just like the previous game, only the wheelbarrow is pushed along a trail of food items, such as grapes, marshmallows, etc. The "wheelbarrow" must eat each item along the way.

WILD WHEELBARROW RELAY

This relay requires one or more *real* wheelbarrows. Team members pair off, with one person pushing the wheelbarrow and the other riding in the wheelbarrow. They must travel around a goal and back; however, the wheelbarrow driver is blindfolded and the person sitting in the wheelbarrow must give him directions.

8.

QUIET GAMES

All of the games in this chapter are designed for use with groups in a confined area, such as the living room of someone's home, and require relatively little physical activity. They are ideal for parties or for warm-ups before a meeting or activity.

Also included in this chapter are thinking or word games that require answering questions; table games that are usually played around card tables; and mindreading games that requires some mental gymnastics to figure out how the game is played.

ADD-A-LETTER

This game works best with a group of fifteen or less. Have the group sit in a circle. One person begins to spell a word, giving a letter. The next person adds another letter, each person attempting to add a letter without completing a word. A person gets a mark against him (you can possibly mark on their hand with a marker of some kind) whenever he accidentally finishes a word or is forced to say the last letter in a word. A person is out of the game when he gets five marks. A person can fake a letter (doesn't really have a word in mind) when it seems he is forced to finish a word. If the next person thinks he is faking, he can challenge. If he catches the person who is bluffing, the bluffer gets a mark. If the person challenged can give the word he had in mind, then the challenger gets a mark. The winner is the last person left in the game. All words must be legitimate words, verifiable in a college-level dictionary.

ANATOMY TWISTER

Here's a good game for small groups that is patterned after the old Twister game, which has been so popular for years. To play, you'll need to make two sets of dice. (You can do this by using children's blocks.) Each pair of dice will have one die numbered one through six (like a normal die) and the other has six parts of the body either written or drawn on the die.

Teams can consist of eight people—six to comply with the instructions and two to roll the dice and give the instructions. Each roller gets one numbered die and one anatomy die. The other six members of the team number off. To start the game, just roll the dice.

Here's how the game could go: The first roller tosses a #3 on the number die and a "nose" on the anatomy die. The other roller tosses a #6 on the number die and "foot" on the anatomy die. So team member #3 must hold his nose in team member #6's foot. They must hold this position until this round is over as well as comply with any further instructions that come up on subsequent tosses of the dice. For example, if a succeeding roll of the dice requires #3 to place his nose somewhere else, then an attempt is made to position the nose in *both* places at once. A later roll of the dice does not cancel out an earlier roll of the dice.

The winning team is the one that can successfully accomplish the most rolls of the dice before reaching the point of physical impossibility or exhaustion. Of course, with most youth groups physical impossibilities don't exist. You can also play this game without team competition—just for fun.

ANIMAL RUMMY

For this game, give everybody a sheet of paper and a pencil. Then, have everyone write the same name at the top of the paper, each letter to head a column, like this:

H	U	B	E	R	T

The leader now calls, "Animal," and each player begins writing the names of as many animals as he can in each column with the first letter of the animal matching the column letter (for example, elephant for E). After a set time limit (two minutes is usually plenty of time), the leader asks for all the animals listed in each column and makes a master list. Players receive points for each animal they have listed, plus a bonus point for each animal not listed on anyone else's sheet. Various categories, such as flowers, vegetables, trees, or cities can be used.

APRIL FOOLS GAME

At the beginning of a party or special event, give everyone in the room a card with an instruction written on it. The instruction is an April Fools trick that they must play on someone before the party is over. For example, it might be "Tell someone that his fly is open" or "Tell someone that there is a phone call for him." If the person falls for it (looks down, goes to get the phone), then that person has been officially fooled and is out of the game. The idea is to avoid being fooled but to fool as many others as possible. Check at the end of the party how many people were fooled, who fooled the most people, and so on. This game plays best when there is plenty of time and other things happening as well. It's fun!

ASSASSINATION

Here's a good thinking game that's a lot of fun. You will need two leaders (or referees). The leaders divide the group into two teams and explain that each team represents a country. In each country, everyone will be loyal citizens, except for one person who will secretly be a spy for the opposing enemy country.

Then the two countries move into separate rooms, where they cannot be heard by the enemy country. There each must choose a king who will be unknown by the enemies. After choosing a king, a spy will also be chosen from among the other members of the country by a secret drawing of cards, so the members will not know which one is the enemy spy. To choose the spy each leader has all the members of one country, except the king, draw slips of paper from a bowl, look at it, and then give it to the leader to see. All slips, except one, will have "Loyal" written on them; the one other slip will read "Spy."

While the countries are still separated, the two leaders switch rooms and tell each country the name of their spy on the other team but not the name of the other country's king. Then the two countries are brought into the same room. The object is for each country to find out from their spy who the other country's king is and to assassinate him. Assassination is done by stabbing the enemy with one's finger—in his back only (or whatever method you choose). If they mistakenly assassinate someone who is not the king, they lose the game.

Each team knows their spy, but they do not know which of their own members is the enemy spy. If they can find him, they can assassinate him, too. However if they assassinate one of their loyal members, they lose the game.

The spies may use any method they wish to tell their friends on the other team who the king is. But the spies should be subtle, lest they give away their identity and are assassinated. Likewise, the country members should be careful to keep secret who the spy is among them. The country that assassinates the other country's king first is the winner.

BANG, YOU'RE DEAD

This is a game where the leader knows the secret, and the rest of the group try and guess how it's done. Make sure that the group understands it is possible to know right away who has been shot, but they have to figure out what the secret is. Everyone should be seated around the room in a casual manner, with the leader at the front. After everyone is quiet, the leader raises his hand and points it like a gun and says, "Bang, you're dead." Then he asks, "Whom did I shoot?" It's hardly ever the person who was being pointed at. Several people will guess, and they will most likely be wrong. Then the leader announces who it was. The leader continues to shoot people but changes what he does each time.

And just what is the secret? The person who was actually shot is the first person to speak after you say, "Bang, you're dead." Sooner or later, someone will catch on or perhaps the leader will make it a little more obvious, which only baffles the rest of the group even more. It's fun as well as frustrating.

BITE THE BAG

Stand a grocery bag in the middle of the floor and ask everyone to sit in a wide circle around it. One-at-a-time each person comes to the bag and tries to pick it up *only* with his teeth (only the bottoms of his feet can touch the floor), then stands up. As you go around the circle, you will observe that almost everyone can do this. After everyone has had a turn, cut off or fold down an inch or two of the bag. Go around again. With each round, shorten the bag. When a person is no longer able to pick up the bag and stand up, he is out. The winner is the only person who can pick it up without falling.

BOARD-GAME ROTATION

Here is a good way to have an evening of board games without being bored. Set up tables in a circle with a different two-player board game on each table. Put chairs on two sides of the table with half the chairs facing out and half the chairs facing in toward the circle.

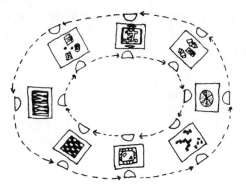

Have everyone take a seat. The games begin and end at the whistle (after about five minutes). Both circles rotate to their right, so each person moves to a different game with a different opponent. The games, however, are not reset, but the new players just take over where the last players left off. So a person might move from a winning Checkers game to a losing position in Yahtzee.

Each game is worth a set amount of points, and the circle (or team) is given credit for the win, then the games are started again. This game works well as a mixer since everybody plays against almost everybody else.

Here are some other tips: Large groups may need several circles. Four-person games like Rook or Monopoly can be used, but you would need to set up a more complex rotation. Use games that everyone already knows how to play or games that are simple enough to teach easily at the beginning.

BUZZ

For this game, the group should be seated in a circle. Begin counting in rhythm around the circle from one to one hundred. Whenever someone comes to a number containing a *seven* or a *multiple* of seven, he says, "Buzz," instead of that number. For example, it would go 1, 2, 3, 4, 5, 6, *buzz*, 8, 9, 10, 11, 12, 13, *buzz*, ,15, 16, 17, 18, 19, 20, *buzz*, 22, etc. You have to stay in rhythm, and if you make a mistake or pause too long, you are out or you must go to the the end of the line.

You can also play FIZZ—the same game, except the number is five instead of seven. This game is easier for younger kids. To really get complicated, play FIZZ-BUZZ, which would sound like this: 1, 2, 3, 4, *fizz*, 6, *buzz*, 8, 9, *fizz*, 11, 12, 13, *buzz*, *fizz*, 16, 17, 18, etc.

CHARADES GAMES

The old game of charades is always a winner with small groups in a living room setting. Divide the group in half and have each side write names or titles (of books, films, songs, etc.) on slips of paper for the other half to pantomime, or think of them ahead of time yourself. Mix up the papers in a hat. Then, each player draws a title from the hat and gives it to the other team, and they patomime it. Appoint a timekeeper for each team and set a time limit of three minutes for each player. The team with the least time is the winner.

Here are some other variations:

1. ART CHARADES: This is like regular charades, only each side is given a large drawing pad and a felt-tipped marking pen. Each player draws his song, book, or movie title (without using any letters, numbers, or words) and tries to get his team to guess what he's drawing. This is a good game for Christmas, using Christmas carols and songs.

You can make this a faster-moving game by making two identical sets of about twenty titles and giving one set to each team. On "go," one player on each team picks a title out of the hat and keeps drawing it until it is guessed by the team, then the next player quickly selects a title, and so on until all twenty titles have been guessed. The team to guess all twenty titles first is the winner.

2. HIP CHARADES: This is played just like charades, except that team members spell out (or write) words in the air with their *hips*. The team shouts each letter as they recognize it and attempts to guess the correct title in the fastest time possible. The results are hilarious.

3. VALENTINE CANDY CHARADES: This one, of course, is best for a Valentine's Day party. Get a package of candy conversation hearts that have two or three word sayings, such as "I Love You," "Slick Chick," "Turtle Dove," etc. Each player picks one of the candies from a bowl, and using the regular rules for charades, tries to pantomime the message. Whoever correctly guesses the saying gets to eat the candy. You can use teams or just have each person do it for the whole group. It's hilarious to watch kids try to act out phrases like "Lover Boy," "Kiss Me," and all the other crazy sayings they put on those traditional candies.

4. OCCUPATIONAL CHARADES: Each player tries to pantomime a particular occupation or ambition. Make up a list of creative ones, such as rock singer, Miss Universe, an astronaut, a chimney sweep, an elephant trainer, etc.

CHOCOLATE-BAR SCRAMBLE

Here is a great game for groups of six to ten. Place a chocolate bar in the center of the table. The candy should stay in its wrapper and, to make the game last longer, you could wrap the candy in giftwrapping paper as well. Each person sitting around the table takes a turn at rolling the dice. The first person who rolls a six gets to start eating the candy bar— but *only* after he puts on a pair of mittens, a cap, a scarf; *only* after he runs once around the table; and *only* with a knife and fork.

While he is getting ready (according to the instructions above) to eat the candy bar, the group keeps taking turns rolling the dice. If someone rolls a six, then the person who rolled the six before him relinquishes his right to the candy bar, and the second person must try to eat the candy before someone else rolls a six. The game is over when all the candy bar is devoured or when everyone drops to the floor from exhaustion.

CONFUSION LANE

Have the kids sit in a semicircle (like a horseshoe). The person on one end takes a pencil and hands it to the second person and says, "Here is a pencil." The second person says, "A what?", and the first person repeats, "A pencil." The second person hands the pencil to the third person, and says, "Here is a pencil," and the third person says, "A what?" The third repeats, "A pencil," and the second person tells the third person, "A pencil," and so on all the way around the semicircle. The hard part, however, is that you start a different item in the same way from the other end of the line. When they meet in the middle, chaos breaks loose.

COOTIE

Here's a fast-moving game that accomplishes a lot. Not only do the kids have a great time, but they end up meeting and having fun with almost everyone in their youth group by the time the game is over.

Have a number of card tables set up with one pair of dice per table, a good supply of score sheets (see example), and four pencils. Before everyone arrives, arrange the tables in a large circle or a pattern that will allow movement from a lower number table to the next higher number table. The tables should be numbered consecutively with the #1 table considered the highest numbered table. After the group arrives, make sure all the tables are full and remove any extras. Give each person a score sheet and have him write his name on the upper right corner.

The game is ten rounds long. At the beginning of each round, the people sitting across from each other are automatically partners for that round only. The partners then trade score sheets at the beginning of each round to draw the cootie for the other while he rolls the dice.

Every table begins playing the game at the same time. Each person takes a turn rolling the die as rapidly as possible. The numbers on the die correspond to parts of the cootie's body (see score sheet), so a #2 must be rolled first before any other part of the body can be drawn. If a person rolls a number he can use, he keeps rolling until he rolls a number he can't use and passes the die to the next person. When one person has rolled all the numbers needed to finish his cootie, then he uses his turn to roll for his partner. When both partners have completed their cooties, they shout, "Cootie," and the round is over. Play stops at all tables, regardless of how far along everyone else is.

	Number on Dice	Points	
	1 — Head	= 1	
	2 — Body	= 2	
	3 — Eyes	= 6	
	4 — Ears	= 8	
	5 — Tail	= 5	
	6 — Legs	= 36	

All partners trade score sheets and have sixty seconds to add up their score and move to a new table, if necessary. Movement between rounds is as follows: The people with the highest score at each table move to the next highest numbered table (e.g., from #4 to #3). People with the lower scores at each table remain at that table. (Exception: The winners at the #1 table remain and the losers at the #1 table move to the last table.) No one can play with the partner they had in the previous round. The Great Cootie (winner) is the person with the highest total score for all ten rounds.

CONTAGIOUS GAME

Stand or seat kids in a circle, so all can see each other. The person on the end starts by describing his ailment. For example, he might say, "My right eye twitches," and everyone in the group starts twitching his right eye. The next person might say, "My left foot has the jumps," or "I have whooping cough," and everyone must start doing what he says. After a few people share their ailments, everyone should be jumping, twitching, coughing, sneezing, and having a great time.

CUT THE CAKE

Fill a small bowl with flour and pack it tight. Turn it upside down on a T.V. tray or baking sheet, remove the bowl, and leave only the flour mold. Now put a cherry on top. The group gathers around the cake, and each person takes a knife and "cuts the cake," slicing off any size piece they choose. The knife passes all around the circle. The more the cake is cut, the closer each person gets to the cherry on top. Whoever cuts the slice that makes the cherry fall must pick up the cherry with his teeth (no hands) and eat it.

DICE DIVE

Here's a wild living-room game for small groups. For larger groups, divide into smaller groups and get several games going at once.

Have players sit in a circle and number off 1-2-1-2, so every other player is on the opposite team. Place a pile of marbles on the floor in the center of the circle of kids. There should be about six to ten marbles per player.

Begin with any player. He throws a pair of dice onto the floor. If the total is *even* nothing happens. But if the total is *odd*, everyone must dive for the marbles and grab as many as possible until all of them are gone. Points are totaled (one point for each marble grabbed by your team), and the marbles returned to the pile.

Now a player on the opposing team throws the dice. Turns alternate between team members until everyone has had a chance to throw. Then the game is over, and the team with the biggest total wins.

If anyone grabs the marbles when the dice throw is *even* (it will happen frequently), all marbles grabbed must be deducted from the offending team's current total. The game gets frantic as players try to anticipate the roll of the dice, so it's a good idea to draw a line around the marbles and have everyone stay behind that line until the dice hit the floor.

DICTIONARY

Dictionary can be played by any number of people. All that is needed is a dictionary and a pencil plus a 3 X 5 card for each player.

One person looks up a word in the dictionary that he thinks no one will know. Then he asks the group if anyone knows the definition (to make sure no one does). He copies the correct definition on a 3 X 5 card and then asks each player to write as good a definition of the word as possible on his own card and sign it.

The phony definitions are all collected and read to the group, along with the correct one, which is mixed in with the others. The object is to guess the correct one. A point is given to each player who guesses the right definition. A point is also given to each player for every person who thinks his (wrong) definition is the correct one. The person choosing the original word is given five points if no one guesses the correct answer.

ELEPHANT, RHINO, AND RABBIT

The players sit in a tight circle with IT in the middle. IT points to someone in the circle and says either, "Elephant," "Rhino," or "Rabbit." The person he points to must either put his hands behind his back for "Rabbit," put his hands in a fist in front of each other in front of his nose for "Elephant," or he must put both fists on his nose with the two index fingers pointing upward for "Rhino." The two people on either side of the player pointed to must put an open hand facing IT to the player's head for "Elephant" (like elephant ears). For "Rhino," they must put a fist to the other's head (like rhino ears). For "Rabbit," they must put a fist to the head with one finger pointing upward (like rabbit ears). All of this must be done before the count of ten. If any one of the three people fails to do his part, he then becomes IT.

ENDLESS WORD

Have the group form a circle. The first player says a word and then counts to five at a moderate speed. Before he says five, the player to his right has to say another word that begins with the last letter of the word just said, and so on around the circle. No one is allowed to repeat a word that has already been spoken. It is counted as a miss if the player can't think of a word before the other player says, "Five." Two misses (or one if it's a large group), and the player is out. If it is a first miss, he starts again with any word. If no one is getting put out, have the player count to five more rapidly; if everyone is getting out, have him count to ten or fifteen. This game is a lively one, and you'll soon find out who is out to "get" the person next to him.

FARKLE

The object of this game is to score as much *over* five thousand points as possible by throwing six dice. Points are scored in this manner:

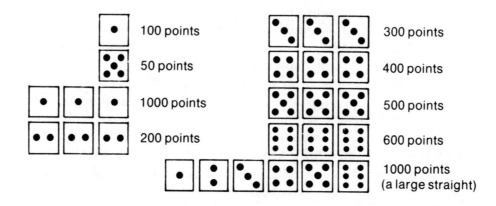

Any three of a kind or large straight must be rolled in one roll, not accumulated in more than one roll. The player starts by rolling all six dice. After rolling, he has the option of ending his turn and adding the score of his dice to his accumulated game score or putting aside one or more of his dice that score and rolling the remaining dice. He may continue to do this until he either decides to stop or scores nothing on the dice he rolls. Any time a player rolls dice and scores nothing on the dice he rolls, he immediately loses his turn and all points accumulated on that turn—a Farkle. Whenever he ends up with all six dice scoring points, whether in one turn or in several, he has "turned them over"— he may roll all six again and add to his accumulated score that turn until he chooses to stop or farkles. If he farkles, he loses *all* points accumulated on that turn, including those before he turned them over. Thus, a player's score is not added until he chooses to stop. Once a player sets aside a scoring die or dice, he may not roll them again until he turns over all six dice. A player's *first* score to get into the game must be at least 500 on that turn. If he doesn't score 500 points before he farkles, he must try again on his next turn. Play goes around the circle until a player accumulates five thousand or more points. At this point, his game is over, and everyone else has only one more turn—a last chance to pass him. Whoever ends then with the highest score wins.

This is a good party game because any number can play, it's simple, and it promotes conversation. Farkle also tests the balance between a player's greed and good judgment!

FICKLE FEATHER

Spread a sheet out flat on the floor. Have all kids kneel around the sheet on all four sides of it, then pick up the sheet by the edges, and pull it taut, holding it under their chins. A feather is placed on the sheet, and the kids blow the feather away from their side. Each side of the sheet is a team, and if the feather touches one of the team members or gets blown over their heads, that team gets a point. The team with the fewest points is the winner.

FINGERS UP

Have the kids pair off and face each other with their hands behind their backs. On the count of three, they hold both hands in front of their faces with a certain number of fingers on each hand held up. A closed fist means zero on that hand. The first person to say the total number of fingers up on all four hands wins the game. Each pair should go for the best two out of three.

After everyone has done this, all of the losers sit down on the floor, and all the winners pair off again and play the game among themselves, and so on until there is a championship match between two people. This game requires quick thinking and is a lot of fun to play.

FLEA MARKET

This is a good party game. You will need to prepare ahead of time a large number of one-inch square pieces of paper, all different colors, some with numbers on them. These are hidden all around the room. At the signal, all the group hunt for the squares, and as soon as they have been found, kids start trading with each other, trying to acquire the colors they think are worth the most. The value of the colors and numbers is unknown to the players until the trading is over. Then announce the values, and whoever has the most points wins. Another variation is to use this as an Easter Egg Hunt.

Colors: White = 1 point   *Numbers:* 7 = add 50
                     Brown = 5 points   11 = double score
                     Green = minus 5   13 = subtract 50
                              points   15 = add 1
                     Blue = 2 points   etc.
                     Red = 10 points

GEIGER COUNTER

For this game, everyone is seated casually around the room. The leader selects a volunteer to leave the room. While he is away, the group agrees on a hiding place for a random object, which the leader hides. The person returns and tries to find the object, not knowing what the object is. The rest of the group, much like a Geiger counter, "tick-tick-

tick-ticks" *slower* as he moves away from the object and *faster* as he moves closer, until the object is found. Time each player to see who can find the object in the fastest time.

GUESS THE INGREDIENTS

Here's a simple quiz game to give your kids. Copy the ingredients of a few common items from   r refrigerator. Pass this list out to your kids and have ther   ach item is. Here are a couple of examples:

1. Soybean oil, eg   r, salt, sugar, and lemon juice (mayonnaise).
2. Tomatoes, vine   salt, onion powder, and spice (ketchup).

HELP YOUR NE

Here's a simple card   . You need a minimum of four pec   m. If you have lots of kids, get lots   d one deck of regular playing card   cards) for each four people who pl

Everyone gets o   rs two through twelve (Jack is elev   and the Ace are not used. The card   n front of each person.

The first playe   es a pair of dice and rolls them. W   r then turns over the corresponding   comes to seven, then the player turns over   .

The player keeps rolling as long as he has cards to turn over. He can, however, turn over the cards of the player to his left to keep his turn alive—"help your neighbor." His turn continues until he can no longer turn over any cards from either his hand or his neighbors. The game ends when a player has turned over all of his cards.

HIDE THE LOOT

Make two counterfeit one-million-dollar bank notes and hand one each to members of two teams. After one team leaves the room (the treasury agents), have the other team (the counterfeiters) select a place to hide the counterfeit note.

The treasury agents are invited back to ask questions that can only be answered "yes" or "no." Each treasury agent is allowed to ask as many questions as he wishes; however, the questions must be directed to one specific counterfeiter who must answer truthfully and must be about how the note was hidden and what the note is touching in its hiding place, not about the specific hiding place itself. For example, he may ask, "Did the person who hid the note have to stand on tiptoes or on a chair to reach the hiding place?" or "Is the note lying directly under something?" The agents are not allowed to walk around the room during their questioning.

Whenever an agent decides to guess the hiding place, he must announce that he is guessing. If he guesses wrong, he is eliminated from the game. After the hiding place is guessed, the teams switch roles, and the game continues.

The object of the game is either to eliminate all of the agents or keep them asking questions. If one team is able to eliminate all the agents and the other team cannot when the roles are switched, then the first team is the winner. Otherwise, the winner is whichever team forces the other team to ask the most questions before the hiding place is guessed.

HOT POTATO

Most toy stores carry a children's game called "Spudsie, The Hot Potato" (a red plastic potato that winds up). After about fifteen seconds, a bell inside the potato rings. The object of the game is to pass the hot potato around the group without having the bell ring when you're holding it. Two rules should be announced—no throwing the potato and no refusing to accept the potato if it is handed to you. It's a lot of fun with small groups of any age. You can play an elimination-type game, with each loser eliminated from the next round (they can sit on the floor) until only two people are left, and a winner is finally declared. A variation is to use the hot potato to select volunteers for other activities.

HOW'S YOURS?

For this game, everyone is seated around the room and one player is asked to leave. While that player is out, the group chooses a noun (like shoe or job) to be guessed by the absent player. When the player returns, he asks, "How's yours?" to anyone he chooses. That person must respond with a true answer (one word adjectives are sufficient), describing the mystery noun that is *theirs*. For example, if the noun is car, someone might answer, "old" or "expensive." The player tries to guess the noun after each adjective until he guesses correctly. The last player to name an adjective before the correct noun is guessed becomes the new player. It's fun and good for a lot of laughs.

IRONGUT

If you have some daring kids in your group, try this contest. Prepare a concoction using fifteen to twenty-five ingredients (see sample list below) found in any kitchen and carefully list all the ingredients. At your meeting, call for some volunteers to be the Irongut. If teams are already formed, choose one or two from each team.

catsup	vinegar
mustard	orange juice
horseradish	tartar sauce
cinnamon	paprika
nutmeg	oregano
garlic	soda
milk	pepper
salad dressing	hot sauce
pickle juice	Worcestershire sauce
onion salt	salt

Those who are brave enough to accept the challenge take turns tasting the potion, which is usually a thick, yucky brown brew. The winner is the person who can list the most ingredients used. Keep a close watch on the kid who asks for seconds!

KILLER

This is a very popular game, which your kids will love. Everyone sits in a circle (in chairs or on the floor) and faces the center. The leader has a deck of playing cards and lets everyone in the room take one card *without* showing it to anyone. (There are only as many cards in the deck as there are people in the room.) One of the cards is a Joker, and whoever draws it becomes the killer. No one, of course, knows who the killer is except the killer himself. Play begins with everyone just looking around at each other and talking casually. The killer *kills* people by *winking* at them. When a person notices that he has been killed (winked at), he waits ten seconds, then says, "I'm dead." The object is to guess who the killer is before you get killed. Once you are dead, you can't reveal who killed you. If you guess wrong, then you are dead, too. The killer tries to see how many people he can kill before he gets caught. When he is caught, the cards are collected and reshuffled, and the game can be played as many times as you want.

MAP GAME

For this game, get several identical road maps of your state and ahead of time, draw a large number, letter, or symbol, such as number 8, on the map. Make a list of all the towns that your lines cross or come near. Have the kids divide up into small groups and give each group a map and list of towns. On "go," they must locate the towns and figure out (like dot-to-dot) what the towns form when connected with a line—no guessing allowed (a wrong guess disqualifies them). The first group with the correct answer wins.

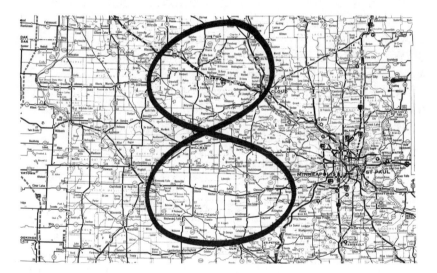

MATCH GAME

This is a variation of the old television game show of the same name. Divide into two or more teams of equal number. Have each team choose a team captain who goes to the front of the room with the other team captain(s). Everyone, including the team captains, should have several sheets of paper and pencils.

The leader then asks the entire group a question (see sample questions below). Everyone, without any discussion, writes his answer on one slip of paper and passes it to the team captain, who has also written down an answer. When ready, the team captains announce their answers, and a point is awarded to each team for every answer from that team that matches their team captain's. Here are some sample questions, but feel free to make up your own.

1. If you were going to repaint this room, what color would you paint?
2. What country in the world would you most like to visit?
3. Your favorite T.V. show?
4. A number between one and five?
5. What book of the Bible has the most to say about good works?
6. What's the best way to have fun in this town?
7. What's the funniest word you can think of?
8. How many kids do you think you will have?

MIND-READING GAMES

The following mind-reading games are basically alike. There are at least two people who are clued in (know how the game is played), while everyone else figures out the secret that the mind reader and the leader are using to perform the trick. As soon as someone in the room thinks he knows the secret, he tries to do the trick. You can keep the game going until most of the group knows the secret or until you decide to reveal it.

1. BLACK MAGIC: While the mind reader is out of the room, the group picks any object in the room. The mind reader returns, and the

leader points to many different objects. When he points to the chosen one, the mind reader correctly identifies it.

Here's how it's done: The chosen object is pointed to immediately after a black object has been pointed to. The name of this game may help give it away.

2. BOOK MAGIC: Several books are placed in a row. One of them is chosen for the mind reader to guess when he returns to the room. The leader points to several books (apparently at random), and when he points to the correct book, the mind reader identifies it.

Here's how it's done: The chosen book always follows any book pointed to that is on the end of the row.

3. CAR: While the mind reader is out of the room, the group picks an object. The mind reader returns and is shown three objects. One of the three is the correct one. The mind reader correctly picks the chosen object.

Here's how it's done: The leader calls the mind reader back into the room with a statement that begins with either the letters "C," "A," or "R." For example, "Come in," "All right," or "Ready." The letter "C" indicates the first object shown; the letter "A" represents the second object; and the letter "R" signifies the third object. So when the mind reader is brought back into the room, he knows exactly which object it will be—the first, the second, or the third.

4. KNIFE, FORK, AND SPOON GAME: In this game, the mind reader leaves the room, and the group chooses one person in the room to be the mystery person. Then, the leader takes an ordinary knife, fork, and spoon and arranges them on the floor in some way. When the mind reader returns, he looks at the knife, fork, and spoon and correctly identifies the mystery person.

Here's how it's done: It actually has nothing at all to do with the knife, fork, and spoon. The leader uses them only as a diversionary tactic. After arranging the knife, fork, and spoon, the leader then takes a seat and sits in exactly the same position as the mystery person. If the mystery person is sitting cross-legged on the floor with one hand on his lap, the leader sits exactly the same way. If the mystery person changes position, so does the leader. The mind reader just matches up the mystery person with the way the leader is sitting. Meanwhile, everyone is trying to figure out how the knife, fork, and spoon arrangement is the clue.

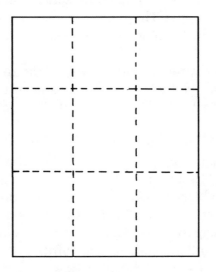

5. NINE MAGS: Nine magazines are placed on the floor in three rows of three. The mind reader leaves the room, and the group picks one magazine for the mind reader to identify when he returns. When he does return, the leader, using a pointer of some kind touches various magazines in a random order, and when he touches the correct one, it is properly guessed.

Here's how it's done: The leader touches the first magazine in one of nine possible places. Where the leader puts his pointer on this first magazine determines the location of the selected magazine in the three rows of three. After pointing to the first magazine, the leader then can point to as many others as he wants before pointing to the correct one, and the mind reader already knows which magazine it is.

6. RED, WHITE, AND BLUE: This is just like BLACK MAGIC, only it is more confusing and almost impossible to figure out if you don't know how it's done. The first time the mind reader tries to guess the chosen object, it immediately follows a red object. The next time it follows a white object, and the third time a blue object. It just rotates red, white, blue, etc.

7. SMELL THE BROOM: The leader holds a broom horizontally in front of him, and someone in the group comes up and points to a particular spot on the broom handle. The mind reader enters the room and smells the broom, sniffing up and down the handle until finally stopping at the correct spot. Everyone thinks that the mind reader has an incredible sense of smell.

Here's how it's done: While the mind reader is smelling the broom, he is really watching the leader's feet. As soon as the mind reader's nose gets to the correct spot on the broom handle, the leader moves his foot so slightly that it is undetected by the group. (The leader should be wearing shoes.)

8. SPIRIT MOVE: In this game, the leader holds his hand over the head of a mystery person in the room, while the mind reader, who is out of the room, correctly identifies that person.

Here's how it's done: Before the game begins, the leader and the mind reader agree on one special chair as the one in which the mystery person will sit. When the game begins, someone will be sitting in that chair, and that person will be the first one chosen. Both the leader and the mind reader note this person as instructions are being given to the group. The mind reader then leaves the room, remembering who was in the special chair. The leader has the group all move to new seats (everyone must change seats each time). After everyone has moved, the leader calls to the mind reader (who is in the next room) and says, "Spirit Moves." He starts moving his hand around, over different people's heads until finally stopping over the head of the person who had been sitting in the special chair. The leader says, "Spirit Rests!" The mind reader identifies the mystery person to everyone's amazement. The mind reader then enters the room to see if he named the correct person, but he is actually looking to see who is *now* in the special chair for the next round.

9. WRITING IN THE SAND: This one is more complicated. The group selects a secret word, and the mind reader comes in and is able to guess the word correctly following a short series of clues from the leader that the group try to figure out. The leader holds a stick in his hand and appears to write the clues in the sand However, the writing does not appear to make sense and bears no obvious relationship to the secret word being guessed. But the mind reader is still able to guess the word on the first try.

Here's how it's done: The consonants in the word (let's say the secret word is "light") are L, G, H, and T. These are given to the mind reader through a series of verbal clues after he enters the room. For example, the leader might say, "Let's see if you can get this one." The first letter of that sentence is "L." That would clue in the mind reader that the word starts with an "L." Then, the leader draws on the floor with the stick, and at some point taps out either 1, 2, 3, 4, or 5 taps to correspond to the vowels—"A" is one tap, "E" is two, "I" is three, "O" is four, and "U" is five. So, in this case the leader would tap the stick three times for "I." Now the mind reader has two letters. The "G" is given next with a verbal clue, like "Got it yet?" As soon as the mind reader has enough letters to guess the word, he amazes the group by identifying the word.

MURDER

This is a great indoor game for casual get-togethers. Place a number of slips of paper in a hat. There should be the same number of slips of paper as there are players. One of these slips of paper has the word "detective" written on it, and another has the word "murderer" on it. The rest of them are blank. Everyone draws a slip of paper from the hat. Whoever drew the word "detective" announces himself, and it is his job to locate the murderer who remains silent. From this point, there are two ways the game can be played:

1. The detective leaves the room, and the room is darkened. All the players mill about the room, and the murderer silently slips up behind someone and very quietly whispers, "You're dead." The victim counts to three, screams, and falls to the floor. The lights are turned on, and the detective reenters the room. Then he questions the players for one minute (or so) and tries to guess the identity of the murderer. If he is correct, the murderer becomes the detective, and a new murderer is selected. During the questioning, only the murderer may lie. All others must tell the truth, if they saw anything.

2. The detective remains in the room, and the murderer attempts to murder as many victims as possible (in the manner described above) before he is caught by the detective. The murderer gets points for every person he can kill before being discovered, and the detective gets points deducted for every incorrect guess. Everyone should get a chance to play both roles. This version is best with at least twenty kids.

MY SHIP SAILS

Have everyone sit on the floor (or in chairs). To start the game, at least two or three people need to know how to play. Explain that the object of this game is to discover, by listening to those who know what their ship "sails with" what their own ship "sails with." Not everybody's ship sails with the same things. The leader begins the game by taking a towel with a knot in it (or a ball) and says, "My ship sails with. . ." (and names something that begins with his initials). For example, if his name is John Doe, he would say, "My ship sails with juicy donuts," (or jumping ducks, jolly doctors, etc.). He then throws the towel to another player in the room, and he, too, must say, "My ship sails with . . . (?)" If he knows how to play, he will say something that begins with his initials. If he doesn't know how to play, he will probably say something that does not begin with his initials, and he must *stand up* until he *catches on* and somebody throws the towel to him, so he gets another try. When he gets it right, he sits down. The idea of this game is to see how long it takes people to find the secret. To start the game, you might tell at least one player the secret.

OPEN OR CLOSED

This is a great game for small informal meetings where kids sit in a circle and pass around a book (or a pair of scissors). When the object is passed, each person must announce whether he is passing it "open" or "closed." For example, he might say, "I received it . . . (open or closed) and I am passing it . . . (open or closed). The leader then tells the person whether he is right or wrong. If he is wrong, he must sit on the floor or stand up (anything to look conspicuous). The idea is to learn the secret, which is: If your legs are crossed, you must pass the object *closed*. If your legs are uncrossed, you must pass the object *open*. It sounds simple, but it is really hard to figure out.

PASSWORD

Password is an old game that originated as a television game show and works well for small youth group meetings. Basically, here's how it's played. You need two teams of two. The best seating arrangement would be something like this one:

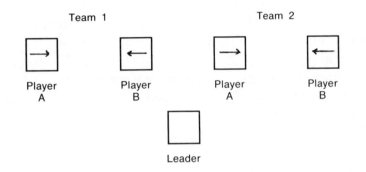

The leader should have prepared ahead of time a number of words (nouns usually work best) written on 3 X 5 cards. After deciding which team will go first, the leader shows the secret word (the same word) to Player A on both teams. Player A on the starting team gives a one word clue to Player B who tries to guess the correct word. If he misses, the other team gets a chance. If they also miss, it goes back to the first team, and so on. Scoring is as follows: five points for a correct guess on the first clue, four points on the second clue, three points on the third clue, two points on the fourth clue, and one point on the fifth clue. If there is no correct guess after five clues, no points are awarded. The game ends when one team reaches twenty-one points (or any score you choose).

The game can also be played with the entire group at once. For example, if you have twenty kids on each team, the seating would look like the diagram on the next page.

The leader has each secret word written on a large card. He shows the card to all the Player A's on both teams but not to the Player B's.

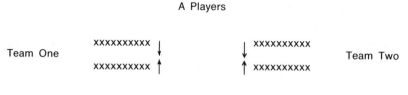

The first Player A on each team gives the first clue to Player B sitting across from him. If they are unsuccessful, then they move to the end of the line, and everybody else slides down one chair. The next time their teams get a chance, two new people try for a correct answer. Other rules stay the same. Alternate Player A and Player B giving clues and guessing in each new round.

THE POINT GAME

Give everyone a score card, then read a list of thirty items, similar to those below. Each person keeps track of his points as specified. The person with the most points wins.

1. Give yourself 10 points if you are wearing red.
2. Give yourself 10 points for every penny you have in your pocket.
3. Give yourself 10 points if you have a white comb.
4. Calculate your shoe size in points, 1/2 sizes get next highest points.
5. Give yourself 15 points if your birthday is on a holiday.
6. Give yourself 10 points if you have ridden on a train.
7. Give yourself 10 points if you have a ball point pen with you, 25 points if it has red ink.
8. Give yourself 10 points if you are wearing lipstick.
9. Subtract 10 points if you are a boy and are wearing lipstick.

RHYTHM

Everyone in the room numbers off in a circle with #1 in the end chair. Number 1 begins in rhythm by first slapping thighs, clapping hands, then snapping right hand fingers, then snapping left hand fingers in a continuous 1-2-3-4-1-2-3-4-1-2-3-4 motion at a moderately slow speed. Everyone joins in the same pattern and keeps in rhythm. (It may speed up after everyone learns how to play.) The real action begins when #1, on the first snap of the fingers, calls his own number, and on the second snap of the fingers, calls somebody else's number. For example, #1 says, (slap) (clap) "one, six," and then #6 says, (slap) (clap) "six, ten," and then #10 slaps, claps, and calls somebody else's number, and so on. If anyone misses, he goes to the end of the numbered progression, and everybody moves up one number. The object is to arrive at the number one chair.

An interesting variation of this game is called SYMBOL RHYTHM. Instead of using numbers, each person uses a symbol, such as a cough, a whistle, scratching the head, etc. For example, each person would do his own and someone else's symbol—slap, clap, cough, scratch head. Still another version is ANIMAL SOUND RHYTHM that substitutes animal sounds for numbers. Either way, it's a lot of fun.

RING ON A STRING

Have the group sit in a circle on chairs. Take a piece of string and have every person hold the string with both hands, except for one person who stands in the middle. Tie the string at both ends to make it one big circle with a ring (large one is best) on the string that can slide all the way around. Have the group pass the ring along keeping it hidden in their hands from the person in the middle who tries to guess who has the ring by tapping different people's hands. When a player's hand is tapped, he opens his hand to reveal whether he has the ring. When the person in the middle taps someone with the ring, they switch places.

S AND T

Divide the group in half—one side is the "S and T's," and the other side the "Everything Else's." Ask everyone to sit and count together as a group from one to twenty, and every time they say a number that begins with an "S" or a "T," the "S" and "T's" stand up. On all the other numbers, the "Everything Else's" stand up. For example, each time the "Everything Else's" stand up at "one," and the "S and T's" stand up at "two and three," and so on. Start slow, then do it again a little faster. The faster the counting the wilder it gets.

A variation is to have everyone sit in a circle and start counting in rhythm around the circle from one to twenty, then start at one again, and so on. Every time a player says a number that begins with an S or T, he must stand up before saying it. If he doesn't stand up or breaks the rhythm, he is out of the game, and the game continues. It's very confusing, but lots of fun.

SPOONS OR "DONKEY"

This game is similar to musical chairs because someone always gets left out. Have the group sit in a circle on the floor (or around a small table). For each player, you will need four cards of the same suit (four Kings, four tens, etc.). The spoons are placed on the floor or on the table equal to the number of players minus one. (If you have six players, there should be only five spoons.) The cards are shuffled, and four cards are dealt to each player. After the players have had a chance to look at their cards, the dealer says, "Go," and each player passes one card from his hand to the player sitting on his right. They keep passing the cards around until one player has four of a kind in his hand. He then grabs a spoon, and everyone else tries to grab one; however, one person will not get a spoon. If the player who first reaches for the spoon does it quietly, then it is often quite a while before the others notice that a spoon is missing, then they all grab.

This game can be played with coins rather than spoons, and then it is called Donkey. Every time someone doesn't get a coin, he gets one letter of the word "Donkey." The first person to lose six times is the donkey. It's a lot of fun.

STINK

Put a dozen numbered milk cartons on a table with various smelly things in each. Cover the top with cheesecloth, a nylon, or something that will hide what's in the carton but still allow the odor through. Let everyone smell and guess what the stink is and write his guesses on a piece of paper. Announce the winner and what the smells are later in the meeting.

Here are some samples:

Rotten egg   Fertilizer
Ammonia   Toothpaste
Coffee   Pizza
Mouthwash (brand)   Paint thinner
Horseradish   Cigarette butt
Smelly sock or gym shorts   Fingernail polish

STORY LINE

The group is divided into two or more teams. Each team elects a spokesperson and then gets a card with a crazy sentence typed on it (the crazier the better). For example, "Fourteen yellow elephants driving polka-dotted Volkswagens converged on the Halloween party." The spokesperson from each group then comes forward with his card. The leader explains that he will begin telling a story. At a certain point, he will stop and point to one of the spokespersons who will have to pick up the story line and keep it going. At the whistle (every minute or so), that spokesperson must stop talking, and the next spokesperson must pick up the story line, and so on for about ten minutes. The object is to work the crazy sentence into the story line and not let the other teams know. At the end of the story, each team must decide whether the spokespersons for the other teams were able to get their crazy sentences into the story, and if so, what they were. Points are awarded for getting the sentence into the story line, guessing correctly whether it got in, and what the sentence was.

TABLE GOLF

This is a good game for socials and parties in someone's home or anytime you want a table game that the whole group can play. Arrange the room with as many small game tables as you have foursomes. Number the tables, making the highest number the head table. Each table has a set of dice that stay at that table, and each person keeps a scorecard with him.

This game is played in nine (or eighteen) holes (or rounds). To begin, the players pair off at each table, so there are two teams. On "go," one team rolls the dice, then the other team, and so on. To begin scoring, someone must roll a six on one or both of the dice. Each player gets only one roll (or turn) unless a score is made on the roll. Rotate rolling the dice around the table, with each person rolling, but when a score is made, both persons on that team get points.

The head table controls the length of the hole. After reaching fifty points, the head table calls, "Stop," and play at all tables must stop. Other tables may have more or less than fifty points on that particular hole.

Now the team that has the highest score at each table moves on to the next highest table. The losers stay where they are, except for the losers at the head table who must go to the lowest table. The winning couples change chairs at the new tables, so they are no longer partners.

A new hole is started, and play continues until the head table reaches fifty points. At the end of the nine (or eighteen) holes, everyone totals his points and, the highest score wins.

Here is how the scoring goes:

Any 6 = 1 point

Double 6 = 25 points

Double 5 = 10 points

Double 1,2, or 4 = 5 points

Double 3 = erases the score for that hole, and you must start over.

TAKING A TRIP

Here's a memory game, which is always fun. Everyone sits in a circle, and the leader begins by saying, "I'm taking a trip, and I'm bringing _____." Anything can be named. The second person then says, "I'm taking a trip, and I'm bringing _____ and _____." The *first* item he names is the item named by the *first* person, and the *second* is a *new* item named by him, and so on around the circle, with each person naming all the items that have already been mentioned plus one more he adds. The game continues around and around the circle until someone goofs it. Give a prize to whoever can remember the most items in the correct order.

THIRD DEGREE

The leader divides the group into two teams—one composed of FBI members, the other of spies. Each spy is given a card bearing one of the instructions listed below; each spy receives a different instruction. The FBI members then take turns asking specific spies questions, calling out the name of each spy before asking the question. The FBI members may ask as many questions of as many or few spies as they choose and may ask any questions, except about the instructions the spies were given.

An FBI member may guess a spy's instructions at any time, whether it is his turn to ask a question or not. Each spy must answer each question always in the manner described on his card. If a spy gives an answer without following his instructions or whenever the spy's instructions are guessed correctly by the FBI member, he is eliminated. The questions continue until all the spies' instructions are guessed correctly.

1. Lie during every answer.
2. Answer each question as though you were (name of adult leader).
3. Try to start an argument with each answer you give.
4. Always state the name of some color in your answer.
5. Always use a number in your answer.
6. Be evasive—never actually answer a question.
7. Always answer a question with a question.
8. Always exaggerate your answer.
9. Always pretend to misunderstand the question by your answer.
10. Always scratch during your answer.
11. Always insult the questioner.
12. Always begin each answer with a cough.
13. Always mention some kind of food during each answer.
14. Always mention the name of a group member during your answer.

Scores are kept for individuals rather than teams. The winning spy is the one who has the most questions asked before his instructions are guessed correctly. The winning FBI member is the one who guesses correctly the most number of instructions.

This game can also be played without teams. Give everyone in the group an instruction like those listed above. Then have each person answer questions from the entire group until someone can guess his secret instruction. Each new question without the instruction being guessed is worth a point.

TRIVIA TIC-TAC-TOE

This game is played similar to *Hollywood Squares*. Two people play at a time. A game board should be constructed out of poster board or cork (bulletin) board, so "X's" and "O's" can be hanged on it.

Old Testament	Sports	Morning Sermon
Riddles	Little Known Facts	Movies
Current Events	Saintly Secrets (Gossip)	New Testament

Prepare plenty of questions for each category. Contestants try to get their "X's" or "O's" three in a row, up, down, or diagonally by correctly answering the question in the appropriate category. If the "X" contestant misses, then the "O" contestant gets to try. For a faster version, if one contestant misses, the opponent automatically wins that spot.

WHO SIR, ME SIR?

The object of this game is to work your way up to the head chair and stay there. Seat everyone in a semicircle of chairs (or benches). Let the group count off; everyone keeps his number for the whole game no matter where he sits.

The game begins when the leader says, "The Prince of Paris lost his hat, and #8 [or any number he chooses] knows where it is. Eight go foot." But before the leader says, "Go foot," #8 has to shout, "Who Sir, Me Sir?" or else leave his seat and go to the end or foot chair (at the leader's right), and everyone moves up a seat to fill his spot. If he says, "Who Sir, Me Sir?" in time, there is a short conversation between the leader and him, like this: Leader: "Yes Sir, You Sir!" Number eight: "Oh no, Sir, not I, Sir!" Leader: "Who then, Sir?" Number eight: "Four, Sir" (or any other number). The leader then quickly says, "Four, go foot," and #4 has to say, "Who Sir, Me Sir?" in time, and so on. Any time someone "goes foot," the leader says again, "The Prince of Paris lost his hat," etc.

Teach the group how to play, begin slowly, allowing one mistake before making anyone "go foot," then gradually speed up. The faster you go, the more exciting the game gets. Kids like to play this game over and over once they get the hang of it.

In case of a tie between the leader and victim, let the group vote if he should keep his seat or "go foot." With experienced players, you can penalize those who say, "Who Sir, Me Sir?" at the wrong time. Players try to get the ones higher than themselves out, so they can move up toward the head chair. Work for a humorous atmosphere, so no one is too embarrassed about going to the foot of the line.

WHY AND BECAUSE
Give everyone in the group a pencil and 3 X 5 card. Have them write a question beginning with the word "why." Collect them. Now have everyone write out answers on cards that begin with "because." Collect them. Redistribute them at random and have kids read the questions they receive along with the answer. The results will be hilarious.

YARN GUESS
This is one of those games you do just for fun. On one side of the room, put some numbers on the wall. Attach to the number the end of a long piece of yarn. Then hang the yarn up the wall, across the ceiling, and

down to a letter on the opposite wall. Let the yarn make a few turns (go through things, etc.) to make it interesting. With about twenty-five different lengths of yarn going across the room connecting numbers and letters, the object is to have the kids try to figure out which number connects up with which letter. Whoever guesses the most wins a prize.

9.

WIDE GAMES

Wide games are games that are generally much more complicated than ordinary games. Teams must plan strategy, organize and assign tasks to team members, abide by any number of rules, and accomplish an objective that may require a good deal of thought, stealth, and skill. Wide games may also have a particular theme, such as spies and secret agents, cowboys and Indians, or armies-at-war. Most also require a lot of space, such as an open field or wooded area with places to run and hide.

BATTLE FOR THE SAHARA

This is a game for two or more teams in an outdoor setting. Each team has a water container and must transport water across the *Sahara* (playing field) to fill the water jug. The first to do so wins. Each team is assigned a color and should consist of (1) a general, (2) a bomb, (3) three colonels, (4) four majors, and (5) five or six privates. For a smaller or larger group, the number of players for each team may be changed. Each player, except the general, has a water cup, and each team has a water jug (a gallon or so).

There is a specified, neutral area where water may be obtained, so players can't get caught while filling up and around the water jug that is located a fair distance away from the water supply—about one to two thousand feet.

Each player, except the general, travels to the water supply area with his cup and gets it full of water. He then travels to the water jug and pours it in. While en route, he may be tagged by a player of one of the opposing teams. A tagging person must also have a cup full of water to be eligible to tag. If a person tagged is of a lower rank, he must empty his cup. If two equal ranks are tagged, they part friends with their cups still full. If a person tagged is of a higher rank, the tagger must tip his out. Each person has an identity card with his rank written in his team color.

All players tag except the bomb (although the private has no use for tagging, being the lowest rank), who carries water. Anyone tagging the bomb is automatically demoted to private and has his cup emptied and must give up his card to the bomb, who turns it in to one of the referees at his earliest opportunity. (This keeps people in the game.)

Any accidental emptying by an opponent gets the offended player a free escort with a full cup to his jug by the offending player. A general doesn't carry a cup of water and is free to tag others at any time.

It is wise to set a time limit, and the winning team is either the one who has the most water in their jug at the end of the time or the one who fills it up first. It is also best to have referees along the route to make sure no foul play ensues and that offenses get free escorts properly.

CHAOS VS CONTROL

This is an outdoor spy game that is best played at a camp where there is plenty of room and good hiding places. It should be played at night and preferably in an area with a lot of trees, high grass, and the like. Divide into two teams—the Chaos agents and the Control agents. (You can name the teams anything. The names are not important to the game.) The Chaos agents try to leave the U.S. by reaching a landing strip where their planes are to pick them up. The Control agents try to capture or eliminate the Chaos agents by hitting them with a club (a stocking full of flour, a newspaper, a paper bag of mud, or a water balloon). The game area should be planned like the example on the following page.

The Chaos agents are safe when in their own territory, but they have to sneak through Control territory to get to the airstrip, located behind Control territory. If they manage to get through, they report to a counselor sitting at a desk on the airstrip. They are safe once they get to the airstrip. When they arrive there, they turn over to the counselor a set of secret plans (an envelope marked SST, APOLLO, etc.). The Chaos team gets one thousand points for each envelope delivered to the airstrip counselor. Chaos agents may then return to their own head-quarters via a path around Control territory to get a new set of plans and try to sneak through again. Control agents may patrol that path to make sure Chaos people are only going back and not coming to the airstrip.

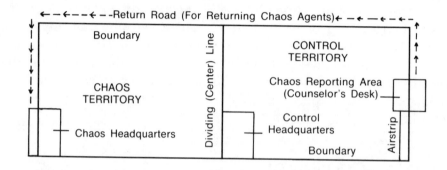

Control agents can only be in their own territory and try to spot and club a Chaos agent. If they hit a Chaos agent, the Control agent takes his prisoner to Control headquarters, and the Chaos agent must give up his plans. The Control team gets two thousand points for each set of plans seized. The Chaos agent is then set free to try again. Adult counselors should keep score, hand out the plans, etc.

You can use several large flashlights (controlled by counselors) to sweep the entire area to give a searchlight effect to the game. The two teams should wear different colored armbands to distinguish them.

DIAMOND SMUGGLING

This is a great wide game that is best played indoors. You will need a fairly large room like a gymnasium. If you are at a camp, use the dining hall or other large meeting rooms.

One room is set up to be a coffee shop in Paris. The coffee shop should be set up like a real coffee shop if possible, with lights low, music, food and drinks being served, card games going on, and the like. Adjacent to the coffee shop on each side are two other rooms—one called *police station* and one called *smugglers' den* or *South Africa*.

Players are divided into two teams—the Diamond Smugglers and the Police. The smugglers meet in smugglers' den before the game begins and choose about a third of their group to be Runners, while the rest remain smugglers. The police stay in the coffee shop.

The object of the game is for the Runners to carry diamonds (marbles) from smugglers' den into the coffee shop and secretly pass them off to a smuggler, who then takes the diamonds back to smugglers' den for points. The Police try to catch someone with diamonds in his possession.

Only the Smugglers know who are Runners and who are Smugglers. Adults in smugglers' den can keep a record of who the Runners and Smugglers are to keep score. The adults issue the diamonds to the Runners and collect them from the smugglers. Only Smugglers may bring back diamonds for points.

The Smugglers and Runners should circulate back and forth into the coffee shop, trying to disguise their actions. Since the Police don't know who are Runners and who are Smugglers, they either have to catch someone in the act of passing a diamond to make an arrest or guess who might be carrying a diamond. Runners can be arrested coming into the coffee shop with diamonds on them, and Smugglers can be arrested on their way out with diamonds, but this can be risky for the police.

Once a Runner brings a diamond into the coffee shop, he cannot return to Smugglers' den with it. He must either pass it to a Smuggler or leave it where it can be picked up later by a Smuggler. Likewise, smugglers may only go into smugglers' den with a diamond that they are smuggling in. For every diamond successfully smuggled by the Smugglers, they get five thousand points.

When the Police make an arrest, they simply go up to a Smuggler, put their hand on his shoulder, and say, "You're under arrest." They are then taken to the police station for searching. They cannot resist or try to ditch their diamonds. The Police officer presents the arrested person at the door of the station to an adult referee who takes the prisoner inside. The Policeman does not go inside. Instead, he goes back to the coffee shop. Inside the station, the adult asks the arrested Smuggler whether he has a diamond. The Smuggler must tell the truth and give up any diamonds he is carrying. Diamonds collected are worth ten thousand points each for the Police. If the arrested person does not have any diamonds, the Police lose ten thousand points for making a false arrest. The prisoner is released, returns to smugglers' den, and gets back into the game.

The Police never know the outcome of the arrest, so the identity of the Smugglers is protected as much as possible. They get periodic point totals, but that is all.

You can adapt these rules any way you choose, that is, play with as many people as you like, for as long as you like. If you discover midway through the game that a particular rule or scoring procedure is not working, change it.

FIGHTERS AND FIENDS

This wide game has certain affinities with the fantasy adventure game *Dungeons And Dragons*, but without the negative elements, such as false gods and demons.

The game has two opposing teams—the Fighters and the Fiends. The object of the game is either to find or to keep the most bags of treasure before the time runs out. Materials needed for the game include a deck of regular playing cards and several bags of treasure, each worth one thousand points. You'll need to make up one bag of treasure for every four people playing. At the beginning of the game, the Fiends hide the bags of treasure.

To begin, the Game Master passes out the playing cards to all the players, so each player has one. There should be the same number of red and black cards, and there will need to be at least one Ace, 2, and 3 of each color in the cards passed out. The cards determine the players' roles in the game and how much power they have. All red cards are Fighters; all black cards are Fiends. Both Fighters and Fiends have Wizards, Assassins, and Zombies on their team (see character descriptions below).

Once the cards have been distributed, and all the players know their roles in the game, the Fiends have five minutes to hide the bags of treasure. There must be at least one and no more than two Fiends guarding each bag. Those guards must never stray more than twenty feet away from the bags of hidden treasure that must be separated by a distance of at least forty feet.

After the five minutes are up, the Fighters head out in search of the Fiends and the treasure. To do battle, the attacking party yells, "Draw," and all must show their cards, with the higher cards winning. In case of a tie, the defender wins. Winners then take the losers' cards, divide them, and add them to their own, making themselves more powerful. After defeating Fiends, the Fighters may look for the treasure. Dead players may not move from the spot where they're killed. If treasure is found, Fighters carry it with them until the game is over. It may be reclaimed by the Fiends if the Fighter is attacked and killed by a Fiend, Assassin, or Zombie.

Here are the character descriptions for each of the players:

FIGHTERS: These are all players with red cards 4,5,6,7,8,9,10, Jack, Queen, and King. Each player's power is the number on the card, with face cards being worth ten. Fighters may travel alone or in pairs. Fighters may kill any Fiends of less power, but they cannot kill Wizards unless they are Forty-point Fighters, and they cannot attack Assassins. Fighters may be killed by more powerful Fiends, equal Assassins, and any Zombie. They may, however, be restored to life (turned into Zombies) by Wizards.

FIENDS: These are the same as Fighters, except they have black cards, and they hide and guard the treasure.

WIZARDS: These players have cards numbered 2 or 3. The color of the card indicates which team they are on. They are worth two or three points, depending on which card they have. The mission of Wizards is to protect players of the same color, restore dead players to life, and to destroy opposing Zombies. Wizards may travel alone or in pairs. A Wizard can only be killed by one Forty-point Fighter, Fiend, or Assassin and cannot be restored to life. Wizards do not attack anyone nor look for treasure. They move around turning their dead teammates into Zombies and killing Zombies of the opposing team. Once a Wizard kills a Zombie, that Zombie cannot be restored a second time. Wizards may, if you choose, put some kind of mark on Zombies that they kill for identification.

ASSASSINS: These are players who have Aces and are worth fifteen points. Red Aces are Fighter Assassins; black Aces are Fiend Assassins. They travel alone at all times. They may kill at will. Because of their point advantage, they are pretty dangerous. In a tie with Fighters or Fiends, they always win. In a tie with another Assassin, the defender wins. They cannot be attacked except by another Assassin. They can only be killed by a Fighter or Fiend with more points, other Assassins with more points, or any Zombie. Once killed, there is no restoration to life for Assassins. Assassins are usually the ones who are most likely to kill a Wizard because they are able to get forty points quicker.

ZOMBIES: These are dead Fighters and Fiends who are restored to life by their Wizards. They cannot attack anyone, but when they are attacked, they may kill any Fighter, Fiend, or Assassin. They may travel alone or in pairs, and they actually try to deceive Fighters, Fiends, and Assassins into attacking them. When attacked, all they have to do is raise their right hand, and the attacker is automatically dead. Zombies can then take the attacker's card(s) to gain points, but they can't use those cards to attack anyone. Zombies may only be killed by an opposing Wizard. Wizards do not collect points (cards).

The game ends at the end of a time limit (forty-five minutes or an hour), after all the players of one team have been killed, or after the fighters have found the majority of the treasure—whichever comes first. The treasure brought in at the end of the game is worth one thousand points to the team possessing it, plus they can add on the points captured in the game (on the playing cards) by all players, dead or alive.

This game can be adapted or changed as you see fit, but there is enough strategy and excitement in this version to make the game one that the kids will want to play again and again. If it sounds confusing, read it through a couple of times for clarity.

FUGITIVE

The group is divided into two teams—the Fugitives and the FBI. The FBI agents are equipped with flashlights. The Fugitives are given several minutes to hide. After the time limit is up, the FBI agents try to find the Fugitives. The Fugitives have a certain amount of time (any time from ten to thirty minutes) wherein they must reach *home base* (or Mexico, etc.), which can be any designated area. If a Fugitive has a light shined on him and has his name called as he attempts to hide or reach home base, then he goes to jail. If the kids don't know each other's names, then the FBI agents can simply call some other identifying trait, clothing, or whatever. If the Fugitive makes it to home base, his team gets ten points. If he is caught by the FBI, then the FBI gets the ten points. If the home base is a cabin, a flagpole, etc., then it would be wise to set a distance of twenty-five to forty feet around home base as *off limits* to FBI agents. To make the game more difficult, arm the FBI agents with water balloons or squirt guns and they must shoot the Fugitives before making an arrest. After one game, play again with the teams reversing roles.

THE GOLD RUSH

This is a rather elaborate camp game that may be played during an afternoon and evening. The entire camp is turned into a *boom town* with these buildings: Sheriff's Office, Assayer's Office, Henrietta's Hash House, Mayor's Home, Prison and Jail, Claims Office, and Bank.

The camp should be divided into nine teams. Each team is given a map of the forest around the camp that is divided into nine claims and asked which claim they want to mine, for example, "Do they want the largest claim, the smallest, the closest to the Jail, the closest to the other claims, the one by itself?" On each claim hide about seventy-five to one hundred pieces of gold (rocks of varying sizes painted gold). Each piece of gold has the claim number on it, for example, the gold on Claim No. 3 has a 3 on it. The gold may be hidden under logs, put on tree limbs, or just scattered in the thickest brush. The claims should be dense forest at least one hundred by fifty yards wide and clearly marked either by trails or toilet paper strung out through the trees.

All the teams then meet in a clearing and select a runner to run to the Claims Office to stake the claim they want. Begin the race with a gunshot, and the runners race to stake their claim—first come, first served—the last one gets whatever is left. After being given the claim slip at the Claims Office, the runners run back to their teams and tell them what claims they have. Then the team goes to the claim and starts hunting for gold. Each team is given a number of potato sacks to store their gold. They have to keep all their gold on their claim till the end of the game. After twenty minutes of mining their claim, a bell is rung, and the teams are now allowed to *jump* other claims—to search for gold not yet found or to raid the main stockpile of another team. All claim jumpers must wear a colored team armband to identify themselves. To encourage claim jumping, award a team double points for gold with another team's claim number.

Each team may defend its claim by using water guns filled with red-colored water. Give each team six guns and two pails of red water. They can only shoot on the claim, not on any trail or road dividing the claim. When a claim jumper is shot, they blow a whistle, and the Sheriff or one of his deputies (the camp work crew or leadership) comes to the scene. All wounded claim jumpers must cooperate once they are shot and are taken by the Sheriff's men to the Prison—two large concentric circles of flour about ten to twenty yards in diameter. The space between the outer and inner circle is *no-man's land*, while the inner circle is the Jail where the prisoners are kept. Several deputies patrol the Prison circumference with water guns and watch for people trying to break prisoners out.

When a prisoner is brought in, put a big "0" on one cheek in indelible ink to indicate that he is a prisoner; his team number is recorded along with his name. His team must break him out within twenty minutes of his arrest by sending a man to run into the Prison to touch him, whereupon both are free to leave. A person trying to break someone out of Jail may not be shot by a deputy till he enters the clearly marked no man's land. He is safe if he reaches the inner circle without being shot. If he is shot, he, too, is made a prisoner, and his team number recorded. However, if a man is freed from Prison by a comrade, he still has a "0" on his cheek and can be shot by *bounty hunters* because he is now a fugitive from justice. He may be shot on any trail, road, or claim, except his own, and the team shooting is given $1,000 at the end of the game for bringing him back to the Jail.

If a team fails to break one of their men out of jail before the twenty minutes is up, the prisoner is released, and a big "0" is painted on the back of his hand to show that he has been properly released. However, his team is charged $2,000 bail for his release. He can't be shot by bounty hunters because of the "0" on his hand. If he is shot while claim jumping again, an "0" will be put on the other cheek, and so on. Thus, it generally pays to break your men out of jail.

Allow the claim jumping to go on for about an hour. Then ring the bell, and the game is over. At the end of the game, each team brings all their gold into the Assayer's Office where it is carefully stored till later.

Now everyone goes to Henrietta's Hash House for a *boom town supper*, complete with an evening of skits, chorus lines, etc. At the end of the evening, the Assayer, with the Sheriff guarding him, weighs up all the gold and doubles the weight of stolen gold. The Assayer can double-cross the teams by throwing out the Fool's Gold whose numbers are in blue paint instead of green paint. He then writes a check for the amount of gold, and the team leader cashes it at the Bank. The Banker can pay off any way he chooses—perhaps in stacks of gold-covered chocolate coins.

HIRED GUN

This game would be good for camps or outdoor events, where there's lots of room to run and hide.

Each person needs a squirt gun or a rubber-tipped toy dart gun. To begin the game, each person writes his name under "R.I.P" on a tombstone-shaped piece of paper. All these so-called tombstones are put into a hat, and everyone draws the name of the person he has been hired to *kill*.

The players go out alone and plan their strategy. When the whistle is blown, the hunting begins. Each player tries to find the person he has been hired to gun down and shoots him. For a shot to be legal, it must be done secretly, so only the victim knows he has been knocked off.

Players must carry their tombstones with them at all times. After being killed, the victim signs his name to the killer's tombstone and is eliminated from the game. Then that tombstone is posted, so everyone can see who is still in the game.

When players are eliminated, they give their tombstones (the names of the people they were trying to kill) to their killers. Those names become the successful killers' next targets.

To give the game a less violent theme, call it KISSER. When a person is shot, he has been *kissed*.

INFILTRATION

This game is best played after dark in a wooded area (or wherever there are no artificial lights). Even moonlight makes this game difficult to play.

Here's the initial set-up for the game. A perimeter is designated along easily recognizable objects (such as trees, fallen logs, rocks, etc.). The radius should be between seventy and one hundred yards, depending upon the size of the group. In the center of the perimeter, a flag is placed. The group is divided into two teams—the Defenders and the Infiltrators.

It is the goal of the Infiltrators to sneak into the area inside the perimeter, obtain the flag, and sneak out, without being *killed* (shot with a flashlight). It is the object of the Defenders to prevent any infiltrator from taking the flag.

All Defenders will need flashlights. (The type with a button that allows short bursts of light works best.) Something designated as a flag is also needed.

Rules For The Defenders:

1. No Defender can enter inside the perimeter.

2. The Defender kills an Infiltrator by shooting him with his flashlight. The flashlights cannot be on more than one second per shot. (No using the flashlights as searchlights.)

3. Any Defender using his flashlight as a searchlight or repeatedly firing his flashlight will be *out of ammo* (out of the game) for five minutes.

4. Once a Defender believes that he has killed an Infiltrator, he keeps his flashlight positioned on him. A judge will check to see if there is anyone there.

249

RULES FOR THE INFILTRATORS:

1. Once an Infiltrator knows that he is shot, he must stand up and identify himself ("Smith, dead").

2. Once killed, the Infiltrator then goes back to the Infiltrators' Cemetery where a judge is to be stationed. The Infiltrator is kept there for five minutes and then allowed to reenter the game.

3. If an Infiltrator believes that the Defender does not know exactly where he is, then he may wait silently until a judge comes to determine whether the Defender's beam is on him.

4. The Infiltrator can be killed inside or outside the perimeter.

This game requires two judges. One judge is located outside the perimeter in the Infiltrators' Cemetery where he keeps the killed Infiltrators out of the game for five minutes.

The other judge is located inside the perimeter. His responsibility is to check out any disputed kills. He does this by going to the spot where the Defender's flashlight beam is located. He declares the Infiltrator dead if he is within the beam. He also gives a warning and then declares, "Out of ammo" to any Defender using his flashlight incorrectly.

At the beginning, a time limit is set. The Infiltrators win if they capture the flag before the time expires. The Defenders win if they protect their flag the entire time.

KAMIKAZE

This is an outdoor game, good for camps or for any group of thirty or more kids. Divide the group into two teams. One team will be identified by blue armbands; the other by gold armbands. Each team has a president who can only be assassinated by a water balloon. The president is seated in a chair that is inside a four-foot circle that is inside a larger circle, some thirty or forty feet in diameter.

The playing area should be divided in half, with each team's president located in their own half of the total playing area. Both teams have offensive and defensive players. The offensive players each get two water bombs (balloons) and may move in any part of the boundaries except for the two circles with the president in the center. No player (offensive or defensive) may enter or pass through the two circles that surround the president.

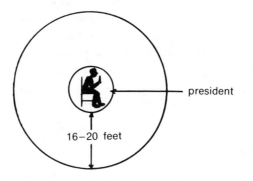

There should be at least four adult judges—one judge each for the team play areas and one judge to watch each president. Another person should be on hand to pass out flour sacks and balloons, so whenever a player uses all his supply, he can get more immediately. This ammo area is safe—no fighting here.

The offensive players try to assassinate the president of the other team by tossing, underhand, a water bomb from the edge of the outer circle. If the balloon hits below the waist, the president is merely wounded, and three wounds assassinate him. If a balloon hits above the waist, the president is killed. An adult judge should determine the legality of the hits.

Defensive players are armed with a small paper bag of flour to defend their president. They can kill the other team's offensive players by breaking the bag of flour on them, but offensive players cannot kill defensive players (they can only run back into their own territory).

251

Defensive players are not allowed into the other team's territory. When a defensive player kills an offensive player, he takes his armband, and the dead offensive player must go to the graveyard (is out of the game). When all of the offensive players of a team are killed, they automatically lose the game.

The game is over either when the specific time limit is up or when the president is assassinated. However, to prevent the game from being over too soon, call a timeout when the president is assassinated and give the teams five minutes or so to reorganize all their players (dead or alive), elect a new president, get new supplies of water bombs and flour sacks, and then resume the game. During the break, scores are taken by the scorekeeper. Assassination of the president is worth two hundred points and armbands of enemy players are worth fifty points each.

PIKE'S PEAK

Divide the group into two teams. Let each team choose a captain. Both captains are then stranded on Pike's Peak located two hundred to three hundred yards from Pike's Dam (a water source). Each captain holds an empty gallon container. Each team member is given a small Dixie Cup. The object is to fill the cup with water at Pike's Dam (the only water source allowed) and then to fill the captain's container. The first team to have a completely full container wins. The object is to stop the other team before they get to their captain by spilling their water or throwing water all over them.

Play by the following rules:
1. Boys can get boys but not girls. (They can run, but no offense allowed.)
2. Girls can get both boys and girls.
3. Within two feet of the captain is a *free zone*, and no combat can take place there.
4. Have neutral people at the dam to fill the cups and have each team fill at opposite ends of the dam.

5. Distinguish teams with colored tape on their foreheads (or any marking device).

SMUGGLER

This is a great camp game that is relatively complicated and requires use of the entire camp area (several acres or so). There are two teams (any number on a team), two territories (half the camp in each), and each team should be appropriately marked (colored armbands, etc.). The idea of the game is to smuggle certain items into the other team's territory (without being captured) and find a *drop*. Points are awarded for successful drops and for capturing smugglers.

The playing area should look something like this:

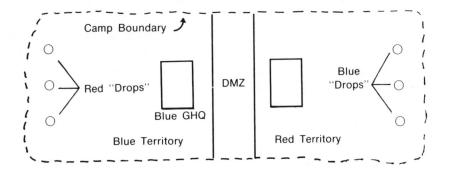

Teams should be designated by color names (for example, Red Army, Blue Army). Each team selects up to 25% of its players (percentages can vary) to be smugglers who are identified with an "S" marked on the back of their hands. They are the only ones who are allowed to smuggle items into the other team's territory and are not allowed to capture anyone. The rest of the team captures smugglers from the other team. Each team also chooses a *general in charge* who coordinates team strategy and remains at all times in the "GHQ" (general's headquarters).

Camp staff and counselors are neutral and called *U.N. Observers.* They are positioned on the two teams' territories to maintain order, offer advice, and make sure everyone is playing by the rules of the game. One U.N. Observer on each side should be assigned the task of keeping score for that side.

One interesting twist to this game is that each team is allowed a certain number of infiltrators (spies who wear the armbands of one team but are working for the other team). These players can be chosen by the game officials prior to the game and secretly informed of their mission. Infiltrators are secretly marked with an "X" (or anything) on one leg (or some other place that is relatively hidden). If accused of being an infiltrator by the team's general, he must show his leg and tell the truth. If a player suspects a teammate to be an infiltrator, the general (because only the general can accuse) is informed and decides whether or not to accuse. Then the accusation must be made in the presence of a U.N. Observer. If the accusation is correct, the accusing team gets five thousand points, and the infiltrator is taken into custody. He must remain in the GHQ for ten minutes and is then released to the team he is working for. He gets a new armband and is back in the game—not as an infiltrator. An incorrect accusation costs the accusing team five thousand points.

The drops are locations (under rocks, in trees, etc.) where a smuggled item may be placed and then declared successfully smuggled. Before the game begins, each team locates their drop positions in the other team's territory, and a game official (neutral person) tells the opposing team's general the location of half of them. For example, the Blue Army might know where half of the Red Army's drops are, but the Red Army isn't sure which ones the Blue Army knows about. Only the smuggling team knows where all their drops are in the opposing team's territory. For example, the Blue Army does not know everywhere the Red Army is attempting to drop items, and vice versa. There should be at least four drops for each side (any number you choose). U.N. Observers should know where the drop locations are.

The *DMZ* is a neutral area that is marked off between the two territories. Anyone may be there without being captured. This is good strategy but optional.

This game should be played at night. No flashlights are allowed. Buildings, trees, and other obstacles may be used for cover. Unsafe areas should be declared off-limits, and players caught here should be penalized by subtracting five thousand points from their team's score.

The items to be smuggled are 3 X 5 cards with the name of the item and its value (see illustration).

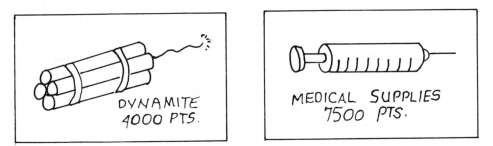

Some items are worth more than others. Points should range anywhere from one thousand points to ten thousand points. There should be more items of lower point value than higher point value (rare items). Any number of items may be used in the game, as long as each team has the same number of items with the same values. The Red Army's items should be written in red ink, and vice versa.

As the game progresses, smugglers attempt to get items successfully dropped in enemy territory. Only one item may be smuggled at one time by a smuggler. Once the drop is successful, the smuggler raises his hand and yells, "U.N." until he finds or is found by a U.N. Observer.

The U.N. Observer then verifies the drop and escorts him back to his own territory where points are awarded. While a smuggler has his hand raised and is yelling, "U.N.," he may not be captured by the enemy. Faking this procedure is a rule infraction that costs five thousand points.

If the smuggler is captured during his smuggling attempt, he is brought to the GHQ of the capturing team and must remain there for ten minutes (time may vary) before being released. He also gets a mark on his hand in the capturing team's color that keeps the capturing team up-to-date on how many times he has been caught. Every time a smuggler is captured, the appropriate score is tallied, and the smuggled item is confiscated.

In the face of imminent capture, a smuggler may dump (get rid of) the item he is attempting to smuggle and hope either that it will not be discovered or that it might be picked up by a fellow smuggler. If the capturing team finds it, they may turn it in for its face value.

Smugglers may be captured any number of ways, depending on how rough or messy you want to get. They may be tagged, tackled, hit with a water balloon, or hit with a nylon stocking full of flour. Choose your own method.

Here is how to score:

1. A successful drop is worth 1,000 points plus the value of the item.

2. An extra 2,000 points is earned if the smuggler can make a successful drop and return to his own team's territory without being captured by the enemy or escorted back by a U.N. Observer.

3. On capturing a smuggler, the capturing team gets points in the following manner.

    a. First time caught—500 points plus half the value of the item being smuggled.

    b. Second time caught—500 points plus full value of item.

    c. Third time caught—3,000 points plus full value of item.

4. Correctly identifying an infiltrator is worth 5,000 points; incorrectly accusing one costs 5000 points.

5. Any item found bearing the opposing team's color may be turned in for the full value of the item.

WAR

This adaptable game is great for camps or retreats where there are several acres or rugged terrain. Any number of kids can play. The group is divided into two (or more) armies—the Red Army and the Black Army (or whatever names you prefer). Each army, under the command of a general, is identified by red or black armbands that cannot be removed during the game. Half the playing area should be assigned to each army as their territory and marked appropriately. Playing time is usually an hour or so, including the armies' organizational time. The object of the game is to destroy the opponent's radar installation by bombing it.

Both armies are divided into two units—the offensive and the defensive. Under the command of a colonel, the offensive unit's mission is to seek and destroy the opponent's radar installation. The offensive unit is also divided into platoons of five to seven members each. Each platoon has a captain and a lieutenant who is second in command. The offensive unit has no boundary restrictions, so they may go anywhere to accomplish their mission.

The defensive unit of each army has the same leadership as the offensive unit, but their mission is to protect their own radar station and to repel the invading offensive unit of the opposing army. This unit may not enter the other army's territory.

The radar installations are two containers (preferably brightly colored) placed on the ground somewhere in each of the two armies' territories. They cannot be camouflaged or hidden, but must be easily visible to the opposing army when they are near it.

Each army gets a specified number of bombs (twenty-five or so). A live bomb is a plastic bottle (or any small container) containing a jelly bean that is the color of the respective army. A deactivated bomb is a plastic bottle without a jelly bean. Only the offensive units of each army are allowed to carry bombs. To destroy the opponent's radar installation, a live bomb must be dropped into it. The defensive soldiers may seize bombs from their opponents and deactivate them by destroying the jelly bean (eating it). The captured bomb may then be activated by the capturing team with a new jelly bean of their own color, which makes their own army stronger. (The more bombs an army has, the better chance they have to get one into the opposing army's radar station successfully.)

Guns (felt-tipped pens) are used, too, and can be taken from captured players. Generals and colonels have two guns each, and each captain has one gun, but no other players may carry guns.

To shoot an opponent, he must first be captured. Capturing a player is done by grabbing him and holding him down (overpowering him any way possible). Boys may capture boys, but boys may not capture girls. Girls, on the other hand, may capture anyone. A captured player is shot by having one finger of his left hand marked with a felt-tipped pen (a gun) and then released. He cannot be pursued for two minutes or recaptured by anyone for two minutes. Also, he may not attack the radar station or one of his opponents for two minutes. A player is dead (out of the game) when he has been shot four times (four fingers on his left hand marked). He then must report to the camp and remain there until the game is over.

A variation is to recycle a dead player by having him wait ten minutes, marking a big purple heart (or another sign) on his left palm, and then allowing him to reenter the game. Then he can be shot four more times (on his right hand).

The game is over when the radar installation has been bombed three times with live bombs. Then a signal will be sounded, and all the players must return to the center of the camp. The losing general and his colonels are then executed by getting a pie in the face.

WELLS FARGO

This game is best located at a camp or wherever there is plenty of running room, terrain, trees, and good places to hide. It is best played with more than fifty kids and can be played with as many as a thousand. Unless there is strict enforcement of the rules and every safety precaution taken, this can be a dangerous game, resulting in injuries. But the risk is usually worth it because the game is one of the most exciting camp games ever created.

Divide the entire group into two teams—the Cowboys and the Indians. Indian headbands, war paint, cowboy hats, etc. help to make the game more fun but are not necessary. In the center of an open field, mark off an eight-by-eight-foot area that is the bank. (A large garbage can may be used as the bank, too.) You will also need to prepare a number of potato sacks filled with rocks that are light enough to be carried by one person or tossed from one person to another. These are the bags of gold. You will also need a piece of tape that is stuck on everyone's forehead (or arms are sometimes safer) and becomes his scalp. Either use two different colors of tape to distinguish the Cowboys from the Indians or mark the pieces of tape with "X's" and "O's." Each player must wear his scalp, so it can be easily seen, not hidden under hats, hair, or clothing.

To start the game, the Cowboys get the gold and have ten minutes to hide out. At a signal, the Indians are released to find them. There are two objectives to the game: (1) For the Indians, to get the gold and to get Cowboy scalps, and (2) For the Cowboys, to get the gold into the bank and to get Indian scalps. The Cowboys try to get the gold in the bank because if they don't, they don't get credit for it. If the Indians can capture it by overpowering the Cowboys who have it, it becomes theirs,

259

and the Cowboys cannot get it back. As a safety measure, boys cannot attack or scalp girls, but girls *can* attack and scalp boys, so it is best for kids to travel in groups and work out their strategies. Once you are scalped, you are dead (out of the game) and must go to Boot Hill.

The bags of gold are worth one thousand points each and must be in the bank for the Cowboys to get points at the end of the game. The Indians get points for capturing the bags of gold and stashing them until the game is over. The scalps are worth one hundred points each. The game can last thirty to forty-five minutes or more. At the end of the game, the teams add up their scores, based on how many scalps they have and how many bags of gold they put in the bank or captured. The team with the most points wins.

WILD WILD WEST

This game is very similar to "Wells Fargo," but there are more teams.

Divide into four (or more) teams. Give each team different colored armbands and give each player a masking tape (or adhesive tape) scalp to be placed on the forehead or the armband, marked to identify his team. The teams are the Cowboys, the Indians, the Miners, and the Outlaws. For more teams, invent more Western-style names and expand the rules.

The object of the game is to find bags of gold and return them to the bank and to kill people (capture scalps). The bags of gold (rocks painted with gold paint) are hidden prior to the game all over the playing area in difficult-to-find places. Just before the game starts, everybody spreads out over the playing area. At the whistle or horn, the game begins. You get one thousand points for every person you kill (scalp you collect), BUT according to these rules:

1. Cowboys can only kill Outlaws.
2. Indians can only kill Cowboys.
3. Miners can only kill Indians.

4. Outlaws can only kill Miners.

Anyone killing a player from the wrong team is automatically dead himself. Boys can only kill boys, but girls can kill anybody. Once a player's scalp is gone, he must go to Boot Hill for five minutes, then he can get a new scalp and reenter the game.

If a player finds a bag of gold, he must get it to the bank to get points for it. A bag of gold is worth five thousand points. Players may steal the gold on its way to the bank by any method they choose. But again, boys can't steal the gold from girls. No player may come within fifty yards of the bank unless he is carrying the gold or is chasing someone who is. The game is over when the time limit is up or when all the bags of gold have been found and turned in for points. The team with the most points is the winner. Another interesting twist is to hide one bag of Fool's Gold (unpainted rocks or rocks with secret marks). Any team that brings it in gets a minus five thousand points.

10.

SPECIAL GAMES
FOR
SUMMER AND
WINTER

The first selection of games in this chapter is ideal for hot summer days because players can get soaking wet. Next are some games for use in or around a swimming pool, lake, or river. Finally, there are a few good games for the winter when there is snow on the ground. Of course, many of the previous games in this book can be played in sunshine or snow, so don't limit yourself to these.

WATER AND WATER BALLOON GAMES

DESPERATION

Here's a wild game, which your kids will love. Two teams get on opposite sides of the room, each staying behind a line. For each round, one person from each team is blindfolded. A squirt gun is then placed somewhere in the middle between the two teams. On "go," the two blindfolded players try to find the squirt gun. Their teammates may help them by yelling directions. As soon as one of the players finds the squirt gun, he may remove his blindfold and go squirt the other player, who is still blindfolded. The blindfolded player may try to run back behind his team's line to avoid being squirted.

Points are scored as follows: Finding the squirt gun—fifty points; Squirting the other player—fifty points; Removing the blindfold illegally (before the squirt gun is found or while being pursued by the person with the squirt gun)—minus one hundred points.

This game can also be played outdoors on a warm day using water balloons.

GIANT SLIP 'N' SLIDE

A giant slip 'n' slide can be made from a large piece of heavy plastic. Station kids at intervals around the edge to hold it in place. Give the kids a grassy lawn, plenty of garden hose, and they will have a blast. Have contests to see who can slide the farthest standing up, lying on his stomach or his back, and sitting down.

HEAVE-HO

This is a crazy version of volleyball. Use a regular volleyball net, lots of water balloons, and two king-sized sheets or blankets.

There are two teams—one on each side of the net. Each team gets a sheet, and the entire team surrounds the sheet, holding it by the edges. A water balloon is placed in the middle of the serving team's sheet, and the team must lob the balloon over the net using the sheet like a trampoline. The other team must catch the balloon on their sheet (without breaking it) and then heave it back over the net to the other team. If it goes out-of-bounds or lands back in their side of the court, they lose the point (or serve). If the receiving team fails to catch it or if it breaks in-bounds, then they lose the point.

The scoring is the same as in regular volleyball. Teams can be any size, but if too many people are around the sheet, it becomes difficult to move quickly. The game requires teamwork and is perfect for a hot day.

MUDDY MARBLE SCRAMBLE

Here's a wild game for hot weather and large groups. Churn up a mud hole (figure approximately one to two square feet per kid). Then work hundreds of different colored marbles into the top five or six inches of mud. (Make sure the mud is without too many rocks.) Each different colored marble is worth a different amount of points. The fewer marbles of one color, the more points they are worth (see example below).

    1 red marble = 500 points
    2 white marbles = 100 points each

25 blue marbles = 50 points each

100 green marbles = 20 points each

Divide the group into teams, each with two leaders—one who washes off the recovered marbles, the other who keeps track of how many of each color have been recovered. At the signal, all of the participants dive into the mud, searching for marbles. After ten to fifteen minutes, the team with the most points wins.

MUSICAL WASHTUBS

Here's a refreshing game for hot days. First of all, find several large washtubs (no small trick if you live in the suburbs). Then fill the tubs with water and arrange them in a circle. Just like musical chairs, have one more person than washtubs, and while the music plays (or at the whistle), everyone marches around the tubs. When the music stops, each person must find a tub and sit in it. The person without a tub is eliminated. One tub is removed, and the game continues until only one tub remains and two people must fight for it. Whoever gets in the last tub is the winner. As the game progresses, it will be necessary to have someone with a hose (or two) to keep the tubs full of water. A variation would be to fill the tubs with mud.

PING-PONG BALL FLOAT

For this relay, get coffee cans (empty), Ping-Pong balls, buckets of water, towels, and one guy with his shirt off for every team participating.

The guy with his shirt off lies on his back about ten yards from his team who are in a single-file line. Place the empty coffee can on his stomach or chest. Put the Ping-Pong ball in the coffee can. Each team has a bucketful of water.

As the game begins, each player one-at-a-time uses his cupped hands to carry water from the team's bucket to the coffee can. As the coffee can fills with water, the Ping-Pong ball rises in the can. As soon as it is high enough, a player tries to remove it from the can with his mouth. The first team to get the Ping-Pong ball out of the can (no hands) and back across the finish line wins.

SLIP 'N' SLIDE RELAY

For this exciting summertime game, use a commercial Slip 'N' Slide or make one out of a heavy plastic sheet. Divide into teams, and give each team member a cottage cheese container full of water. Each person then runs and slides on the wet surface, holding the container over his head with one hand. At the end of the slide, the player pours the water into a bucket. The team that has the most water in their bucket within a given time limit is the winner.

TYPHOON

This game is ideal for summer. Have two lines, single file, facing a water source. At a signal, the first person in each line runs down to the water, fills a bucket, runs back to his team, and throws the water in the face of the next teammate. Before the person can throw the water, his teammate must point and yell, "Typhoon," and so on. The first line to finish is declared the winner. For safety reasons, the water thrower should be at least three feet from his teammates, and a plastic bucket should be used.

VOLLEYBALL IN THE RAIN

This game is also great for hot summer days. Put a pole in the middle of the volleyball net with a sprinkler at the top and the hose hooked to the pole. Then play a regular game of volleyball. It would be best to play on a dirt surface that will become nice and muddy. If played on grass, be aware of the possible damage to the grass.

WATER BALLOON BLITZ

This is simply an all-out water balloon war. Divide into teams, and give each team ten balloons per player and time to fill them all up with water. At the signal, everybody starts throwing water balloons until supplies run out. Anything goes. Judges choose the winner based on which team is the driest.

WATER BALLOON CAPTURE THE FLAG

Play "Capture the Flag" (page 24) with this rule change: Arm everyone with water balloons, and instead of tagging opponents who enter enemy territory, hit them with a water balloon.

WATER BALLOON DODGE BALL

This game is exactly like dodge ball, except use water balloons. Line one team up against the wall and the other team a minimum of twenty feet back. The last person to get hit by a water balloon wins.

WATER BALLOON RELAY

Use as many couples as you want. Each couple race between two points holding a water balloon between their foreheads—no hands. If the balloon drops, they pick it up and keep going. If it breaks, they are out of the game.

WATER BALLOON SHOT PUT

This is a simple game to see who can toss a water balloon (like in a shot put event) the farthest. To give the players added incentive, the youth leader can stand just out of reach of the players, and they use him as a target.

WATER BALLOON TOSS

Couples line up facing each other and are given a water balloon to toss back and forth at the signal. After each toss, they move one step farther apart. The last couple to keep their water balloon unbroken wins.

WATER BALLOON VOLLEYBALL

This game is similar to regular volleyball, only use a water balloon instead of a volleyball and as many people as you like on both teams.

Serve from the back line and allow each team three tosses and three catches to get the water balloon over the net to the opposing team. The opposing team then has three tosses and three catches to get the ball back across the net. The balloon is continually tossed back and forth across the net until it breaks. Then the side where it breaks does not score, but the opposite team gets the point, without regard to who served. Spikes are allowed, but if the balloon breaks on the team that is doing the spiking, the other team is awarded the point. Whichever team wins the point continues to serve until the balloon is broken. Play continues to a score of fifteen, then teams switch sides of the net, and the game resumes. All other regular volleyball game rules are observed, such as out-of-bounds lines, keeping your hands on your own side of the net, and falling into the net with your body.

A variation of this game is "*Blind* Water Balloon Volleyball." To play, hang blankets (or some other opaque material) over the net, so the teams cannot see each other. When the water balloon comes over the net, the element of surprise is added.

WATER BALLOON WAR

This game is similar to "Wells Fargo" (page 259) or other wide games that involve the use of a large area and lots of kids. Divide into two teams and mark players with an identifying color (such as armbands, badges, etc.). Each team has a target person who remains in one spot during the game. The object of the game is to hit the other team's target person with a water balloon.

Each team prepares ahead of time a large number of water balloons (about six times more than the number of players on the team) and keeps them at the team's home base. No player may enter another team's home base to destroy their arsenal of balloons. When the game starts, players on both teams get two balloons each and try to hit the other team's target person. Opposing team members may also kill each other by hitting with water balloons. Dead players must leave the game. The first team to hit the target person wins, and the game either ends or goes into round two. One hundred points are awarded for every dead player and five hundred points for hitting the target person.

WATER BALLOON WHOMP

This game is a great way to cool off on a hot day. Nobody wins, it's just fun to do. Team members each get three to five water balloons each.

Draw a circle on the ground, and one entire team sits down inside the circle, while another team lobs water balloons at them. The sitting team cannot move. The throwing team must stay behind a given line, throw the balloons underhanded on a ten-foot arc. Anybody breaking the rules must sit down on a full water balloon. The teams trade places when one team runs out of balloons. Give a prize to the driest team.

WATER BUCKET RACE

Use an empty gallon paint can, a half gallon milk carton, or a gallon plastic milk carton and place it on a wire (or thin rope) tied at both ends to something solid and over an open space. Divide into two teams and give each team a water hose with water running through it. Whichever team pushes the container to the opponents' end (with water from the hoses) first wins. The water from the hoses just happens to come falling down on everyone involved.

SWIMMING POOL AND LAKE GAMES

ACROSS THE AMAZON

String a rope across a swimming pool and have swimmers race across the pool pulling themselves hand-over-hand along the rope. This race can be done relay style.

AQUATIC BASEBALL

This swimming pool game can be a lot of fun without being too hectic. You will need a rubber ball (or volleyball) and a medium-sized pool. Divide the group into two equal teams. The team that is at bat sits along the side and provides the pitcher. The other team is positioned in the pool.

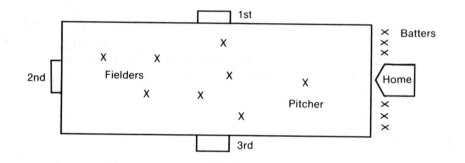

The batter gets only one pitch and must hit the ball with his hand. The batter must swim to the bases, using any course he chooses to avoid an out. Outs are counted if the ball goes out of the pool, if the ball is caught in the air, if the player is tagged with the ball before reaching the base, or if the ball is thrown to first base before he reaches it. The other rules are the same as regular baseball, or you may adapt the rules.

BALLOON PUSH
Have swimmers race across the pool pushing balloons (or anything that floats) with their noses.

CRAZY CANOE
Two people, each with a paddle, sit in a canoe facing each other. One paddles one direction; the other paddles the other way. The winner is the one who can paddle the canoe across his goal line about twenty feet away. It is very difficult to do and hilarious to watch because the canoe tends to go around in circles. In a larger canoe, four or six people can play, with the two teams on each end of the canoe. It is possible to play this game in a swimming pool.

BOAT TUG OF WAR

This is a great game for a water carnival where you have a large pool or lake. Two boats are needed. Tie ropes between the two boats and have them position themselves in the center of the lake or racing area. At the signal, the players in each boat try to reach their goal on opposite ends of the lake or pool. More than one boat can go on each end of the rope (end-to-end) if you have enough boats and room.

CANDLE RACES

For this relay, have players carry a lighted candle across the pool. It must stay lit all the way across.

DINGBALL

This game is played in a swimming pool with a volleyball net dividing two teams. The teams are given every possible kind of ball (Ping-Pong, volley, football, soccer, beach ball, etc.). The object is to throw as many balls as possible over the net, so the opposing team has more balls on their side when the whistle blows. It's a silly game that plays fast.

ICEBERG RELAY

This is a great idea for a swimming party. Players push or pull a twenty-five pound block of ice to the opposite end of a swimming pool and back. It's frigid. Use several blocks of ice and award prizes for the best time.

IN-AND-OUT RACE

Several canoes or rowboats are required for this game. Divide into several teams of five members each. Put each team in a separate rowboat and line the rowboats up evenly in a racing formation. Set up a finish line fifty yards down the course. At the signal, each boat team races toward the finish using only their hands. Whenever the leader blows his whistle, all members of each team are to leap out of their boat and paddle on with their boat. When the whistle is blown again, they must climb back in the boat and paddle it with their hands. Leaders are encouraged to blow their whistles often. After several times in and out of the boat, the boats swamp, and the race becomes a test of nautical skill.

PEARL DIVING

Use marbles for pearls and assign point value according to color. Toss a number of them into the pool. Divide the group into teams and have everyone dive in at once and scoop up as many marbles as possible. The team collecting the most points wins. To add interest, toss in a couple of "rare" pearls that are worth a lot more.

POTATO RACE

This is a relay where contestants carry a potato (or hard-boiled egg) across the pool balanced in a spoon.

SOMERSAULT RACE

Swimmers race across the pool, but whenever the leader blows a whistle, they must stop swimming and do a somersault in the water.

SURFBOARD RELAY

Players line up and paddle to the opposite ends of the pool and back while seated or lying backward on surfboards. Paddling backward is ridiculous and awkward, so everyone has a laugh as well as a good game.

SWEATSHIRT RELAY

The challenge of this swimming pool relay is the changing of a wet sweatshirt. The object is to run through the water to a predetermined point and back, give the sweatshirt to the next contestant, and sit down. Contestants must have the sweatshirt completely on before running into the water. The best way to get the sweatshirt from one person to the other is to have both players lean toward each other and hold hands with arms outstretched. The sweatshirt can then be pulled off one and onto the other easily by another teammate.

TETHERBALL SWIM

This one is really hard. Swimmers swim across the pool relay-style with tetherballs tied to their ankles.

TUBE RACES

Have kids race in inner tubes, paddling backward.

WATER BRONCO

This game is played on a lake, pond, or swimming pool. Tie a long rope to a snow saucer (or any other flat-bottomed object with a handle). Next, get several kids on the end of the rope (out of the water) and one person to ride the saucer (across the pool, etc.) while it is being pulled back to the group. The rider must try to stay in the saucer. Teams can compete for best time or just do it for fun.

SNOW GAMES

INNER TUBE OLYMPICS

This is a good snow sport. All you need is a good slope covered with snow and inner tubes. Make the competition either individual or by teams. The leader is the *only* judge and commentator. The events are these: Men and Women's Singles, Men and Women's Doubles, Mixed Doubles, Stunt Riding, Slalom, etc. Award points for Distance Rode and Form. Poor form criteria: wiping-out, turning the inner tube while riding it down the hill, closing eyes, etc. Stunt riding is based on originality and distance.

MOUNTED MEDIC SNOWBALL WAR

Here's a new version of a very old game—the old-fashioned snowball fight. Divide the group into two teams and play by the following rules:

1. Anyone hitting an opponent on the head is automatically out, even if it was done accidentally.

2. If hit by a snowball, the player must fall to the ground and remain there until his Mounted Medic comes and heals him.

3. Each team is allowed one Mounted Medic who must be a girl, and her horse must be a guy.

4. The Mounted Medic must stay on her horse at all times. She may get off only when she heals a soldier by kissing him on the forehead. A girl is healed by being kissed by the Mounted Medic's horse.

5. A player may only be healed by his own Mounted Medic.

6. Anyone hitting either a Mounted Medic or her horse is automatically out, even if it was done accidentally.

7. Each team chooses one King.

8. The Snowball War is won by assassinating the opposing King, that is, by hitting him on the body, not limbs or head. If the King is hit on the limbs, he must fall to the ground and be healed by the Mounted Medic. The King may be assassinated while wounded. Anyone hitting the King on the head is automatically out, even if it was done accidentally.

9. Option: Kissing may be replaced by wrapping the wounded part with toilet paper.

SNOW PENTATHLON

Here's a wild event for your next Winter Olympics or snow retreat. Divide into teams of eight and set up the following five events. Teams must compete in each event to achieve the best time. The team proceeds from one event right on to the next. Some of these games may be difficult, so take care they are well-supervised to insure safety. You may want to change the rules slightly if a game seems too difficult for your group.

1. STAND-UP-AND-GO: The eight team members are tied tightly together at the waist to form a circle. They begin by sitting on the snow facing out. At the sound of the whistle, they must all stand up together without touching the snow with their hands.

2. SLALOM: Remaining tied together in a circle, they must pass through the starting gate and run (or walk) through a slalom course marked with ski poles stuck in the snow. They must pass on alternate sides of each successive ski pole. If a ski pole is knocked down, the team must return to the starting gate and begin again.

3. TUBE RACE: The team may now untie between two of the team members and stretch out in a straight line. They are given two inner tubes to take to the top of the tubing run and come down the run as a team on the two tubes. Use caution if the run is quite steep or fast because someone could be dragged quite a distance if he falls off the tube.

4. HILL ROLL: While remaining hooked together in a straight line, the team must travel from the top of a small hill to the bottom of the hill without standing on their feet. At the bottom, they may stand up and untie from each other.

5. OCTA-SKI: Use two 2 X 6 pieces of lumber (skis) and attach short rope loops to them at one-foot intervals. Each team member must place a foot through a loop on each ski, and the team "skis" the final distance to the finish line.

SNOW SCULPTURING

This game is great for winter camps or whenever snow is on the ground. Divide the group into teams and have each team find a spot where the snow is good and thick to sculpture anything they want within a given time limit. Traditional snowmen are not allowed. Sample sculptures might include: cars, famous personalities, buildings, cartoon characters, animals, Santa and his reindeer, etc. Encourage the kids to be creative. Judge according to the most creative, the best job, and the degree of difficulty.

TUBECIDE

This game is most suitably played on a snow-covered field with a glaze of ice; however, it can be played on any snow-covered field.

Two equal teams of any size, a field of any size with no boundaries, and two large, well-inflated inner tubes are the only requirements for the game. Each team must be given a goal—two markers fifteen feet apart.

Play by the following rules:

1. Two tubes are placed on top of each other in the center of the field. The two teams form a friendly scrum (arms over each other's shoulders in a circle). The entire group yells, "Scrum" three times. On the third "Scrum," each team attempts to move their tube toward their goal. Teams are on the offense and defense at the same time.

2. When a team gets their tube through their goal, they receive a point. When a goal is scored, play stops for another Center Scrum.

3. The tubes can't be touched with the hands but can be forwarded by any other means.

4. Hooking (putting a leg or arm through the tube and holding it) is not allowed.

5. Checking is allowed, but using hands to push or grab is not allowed.

Keep a patch kit and air pump handy. To handicap a group, give them a larger tube because small tubes are much faster. Modify the rules as needed to keep the game safe and exciting.

ALPHABETICAL INDEX TO GAMES